Teach For Life

Essays on Modern Education
For Teachers, Students, and Parents

Irie Glajar

Also by Irie Glajar, **WE ARE ALL ONE: The End of all Worries**, Scientific and Spiritual Testimonies to the Unity of all Things.

Teach For Life

Essays on Modern Education
For Teachers, Students, and Parents

All Rights Reserved
Published By
Positive Imaging, LLC
9016 Palace Parkway
Austin, TX 78748
http://positive-imaging.com
bill@positive-imaging.com

Cover by **Chase Maclaskey**, graphic design
http://chasemaclaskey.com

No part of this publication may be reproduced in whole or in part, or stored in a retrieval system, or transmitted in any form or by any means electronic, mechanical, printing, photocopying, recording, or otherwise without written permission from the publisher, except for the inclusion of brief quotations in a review. For information regarding permission, contact the publisher.

Copyright   2011   Irie Glajar
ir_gl@yahoo.com
http://the-end-of-all-worries.com

ISBN 0-9842480-4-8

Dedication:

To my family, and to all of you, teachers, students, and parents who care and dare.

Thanks to:

The "Teaching for Success Journal" for publishing some of my articles, which gave birth to the idea behind this book.

Flem de Graffenried for his meaningful suggestions, editing, and praises.

All my students: you taught me so much over the years.

If your Plan is for 1 year, Plant Rice;

If your Plan is for 10 years, Plant Trees;

If your Plan is for 100 years, Educate Children.

Confucius

The aim (of education) must be the training of independently acting and thinking individuals who, however, can see in the service to the community their highest life achievement.

Albert Einstein

Table of Contents

	Introduction	9
1	Why Education	13
2	The Passion of the Teacher	19
3	From Prison to Freedom	21
4	Teach Unity within Diversity	25
5	Create a Meaningful Course Syllabus	31
6	Self-assessment for Better Teaching	35
7	The Use of Student Evaluations	39
8	Grading: Learn to Love it	43
9	Unorthodox Teaching of Mathematics	47
10	Grading Homework in Mathematics?	49
11	Modern Education and Technology	53
12	Education and International Olympiads	59
13	U.S. 'Official' View on International Education	65
14	Religion and Spirituality in Modern Education	75
15	Save Handwriting!	79
16	Humor in Teaching and Learning	83
17	Discouraging Lecture?	87
18	Learning by Memorization	93
19	Teach the Beauty of Mathematics	95
20	Global Education	101
21	Self-leadership for a Better Life	105
22	Question Some Words and Expressions	111
23	Learn to Love Your Life	117
24	Teach Life's Real Values	123
25	Exceptional Educational Experiences	131
	About the Author	135
	Appendix	137

Introduction

Education should consist of a series of enchantments, each raising the individual to a higher level of awareness, understanding, and kinship with all living things.

Anonymous

Academic education is by far the most important endeavor in the formation of a well-rounded individual. Not only does it provide the academic core knowledge but it should also help develop many other traits necessary to lead a productive and happy life. Some of these traits are: personal responsibility, number sense, personal initiative and courage to take risks, common sense, upholding truth, flexibility and tolerance on human issues, open mind, understanding, patience, and the ability to function in a cooperative way in society. Many of these are byproducts of years in the classroom, as students complete a wide variety of well-selected courses, and are also the result of personal efforts toward self-development and self-growth. In this respect, all of us, instructors, students, and parents, are on a path of learning, hence the purpose and the dedication of this book.

We learn something out of every encounter with each other. We, as instructors, learn daily from our students and we need to make sure that our students learn from us as they proceed toward their graduation. However, our students' learning is not limited to the academic content of courses. In every interaction with others we express who we are. An Eastern piece of wisdom says "who you are shouts so loudly in my ears that I cannot hear what you are saying." Our individual personality and character are evident in our interaction with each other and we have the primary responsibility to shape ourselves in the best possible way. This book is a contribution to inspirational sources available in books, TV programs, video and audio programs, on the Internet, together with conferences, workshops, and live presentations.

Consequently, the essays herein deal with a variety of subjects, although I often refer to issues related to the teaching of mathematics since I have been a mathematics instructor in the U.S. since 1982. Some essays are purely academic and some have to do with the philosophy of education from a global perspective. Moreover, several are geared toward self-development, since we, as teachers, students, and parents, all strive for happiness and success in life. The first four essays present my view on education, reasoning around the idea of freedom and personal responsibility in a world marked by a complex interconnection within its immense diversity. The next six essays offer practical suggestions to teachers and are meant to optimize teaching and learning. Essays 11 through 14 cover current trends in modern education such as use of technology, the role of international Olympiads, evaluation of international education in the U.S.A., and spirituality. I continue with five ideas on preserving what I consider valuable from the arsenal of traditional education which are threatened at the expense of 'innovation' in modern times; these include a less accepted reality, namely the beauty of mathematics, tied in with the use of mathematical diagrams. Finally, I conclude with five essays and an invitation meant to illustrate the importance of personal efforts toward self-growth, as we are all intrinsic cells in the body of a living global entity: the human race.

Of course, the subjects included are only a few from a vast number that can fill many volumes. With this in mind, I am sure that all of us, instructors, students, and parents can contribute in our own way to a continued debate meant to improve teaching and learning. One single idea can spark a positive change in the learning process. Students can benefit substantially from constructive contributions implemented by their instructors as they strive to improve. Also, parents can play their indispensable role in the education of their children by being involved at all academic levels beyond the financial support. Therefore, I encourage everyone to search for ideas

Introduction

they can share in the realm of education in order to bring teaching and learning to new heights of success and satisfaction.

I hope this book will enhance the view, the practice, and the perception of modern education. As I offer these essays with love and compassion, assuming responsibility for all editorial imperfections, I wish that the readers will use the ideas within to expand and improve their own approach to education. Especially teachers, who hold the most important occupation of all, should never stop seeking better ways to convey information to students. At the same time, students and parents should be open to different approaches in the process of learning. Agree or disagree with any of these ideas, a rational and civilized debate is constructive. Every one of us should be free to express ourselves for the greater good.

In the spirit of fairness, flexibility, and excellence in education, I envision you benefitting from, and enjoying this book!

1

Why Education?

No calling in our society is more demanding than teaching; no calling in our society is more selfless than teaching; and no calling is more central to the vitality of a democracy than teaching.

Roger Mudd

<u>A Brief Overview</u>

As human beings, we teach and learn every time we interact with one another. We do not only teach what we have formally learned in educational institutions; we also teach, by our example, those ethical and moral values in which we believe. In the light of a multitude of inhumanities culminating with crime and violence, it seems appropriate to look for solutions within the realm of teaching and learning. With this in mind, I think we can safely assume that the undeclared intent of general education is to make the world a safer and better place by providing the knowledge needed to clarify some of our crucial existential concerns.

One fundamental existential question raised by most major cultures of the world is: What is the meaning of life? Or, where is our place in the universal scheme of things? To answer this question we created areas of study meant to investigate our own complete makeup, such as philosophy and religion. However, their fruit is the result of a limited perception of reality if other disciplines are ignored; quantum physics (the subatomic physics of the 20th century, also called the 'new physics'), for example, sustains the view of an internally connected universe. Moreover, the same view is at the core of the major spiritual philosophies of the world. This implies that different areas of life on Earth cannot be considered as isolated any longer. Consequently, in order to optimize the education process of future generations, we should consider a more holistic approach: mathematics, computer science, chemistry, physics, literature, history, government, and so on, should all be presented within a harmonious web (does this word sound familiar these days?). Even more, all disciplines should incorporate philosophical and spiritual components in the respective instructional process in order to present students with possible answers to fundamental existential questions.

The Need for a Holistic Approach to Education

Within this context, modern scientific and medical research together with age-old philosophy and religion maintain that man is a much more complex entity than many suspect. Therefore, why are we here, and why do we do what we do, should be philosophical questions raised also in mathematics, literature, history, nursing, or business management, implying that we cannot teach only the particular nuts and bolts of these subjects anymore. Instead, we should focus on a holistic education in order to evidence the implicit interdependence between all subjects of study. Consequently, to ensure a complete development for all of us, one needs to address the three-fold human makeup: mind, body, and spirit. In a culture so drastically affected by super-fast technological change, which attends mainly to the development of the mind, and secondarily that of the body, ignoring spiritual growth could cause our future to be very dim. The education system is the most important avenue to the future we want, but first, as teachers or parents, we need to enhance our own three-fold readiness, our personal growth, so that we will be able to provide constructive instruction.

Unfortunately, the training received by a majority of graduates from academic institutions is generally limited to the particular degree plan and subject matter. This fact can have powerful implications especially in academic circles by eventually restricting a student's development. In the modern world we, teachers, cannot afford to be partially prepared; we need to realize the magnitude of our impact in the lives of our students at all levels, from pre-K through post doctoral education. Therefore, we can postulate that to become a completely functional human being, people need a broad, holistic, and never-ending education.

To offer sensitive holistic teaching, free of any advocacy for or against any religion, elements of practical philosophy and spirituality should be incorporated in all areas of instruction. Although it is difficult to officially include them in textbooks, we, as instructors, should consider them as adjacent classroom discussion. Of course, this delicate process should encourage an open mind and it must exclude dogmatic and destructive views. It should be connected to the most recent scientific findings, and it should appeal to our common sense. This will ensure an effective implementation of such philosophical and spiritual ideas in our lives through logical understanding and acceptance. More importantly, students and instructors will make these ideas available to an even larger community: that of families and friends. The individual change resulting from such meaningful communication will positively impact our future.

Practical Testimony from a Teacher

As an instructor of mathematics, I would like to offer an example of how effective holistic teaching can be. Ever since I have been connecting my teaching with common sense philosophy in the classroom, students have started to see mathematics as an implicit component of a larger picture. Not only do they approach me at a more open and friendly level, but many also release their old stress and anxiety towards mathematics. They understand the meaning of their math work and how it can enrich their lives. Consequently, grades and retention improve, and attitude positively changes. Students realize now that their old struggles over math problems are meaningless when viewed from a deeper philosophical perspective. Once they understand the origin of my open concern for their educational wholeness and general well-being, students feel more comfortable with math. Simultaneously, they are willing to use my counsel to find solutions to even personal problems that obstruct their academic progress.

Similar goals can be reached in all other subjects of instruction. Instructors can experiment for themselves by considering and addressing philosophical ideas relevant to the subject matter. Bibliography for this endeavor is abundant: bookstores sections (such as Self Growth, Philosophy, Spirituality and Religion), the daily news, personal experiences, and volumes of research in education can provide numerous inspirational themes. Therefore, opportunities for classroom debate can be offered, or at least such ideas can be presented as 'food for thought.' Results can be outstanding.

Finally, why Education?

We guide our lives according to our philosophical beliefs. Every time we learn something new our lives change, even though, sometimes ever so slightly. The philosophy of life we hold today is the product of years of education and experiences accumulated under different circumstances in environments such as family, school, church, on the job, and on the street.

In order to distinguish between 'good' and 'bad' philosophies of life we must examine their fruit. Therefore, we need to ask ourselves: are we happy with our life as it is now? If we are, most likely we had a 'good' philosophical and spiritual inner guidance. If we are not happy, we need to inspect our philosophy by engaging in personal growth endeavors, such that our lives could take a new path. If later on in life a person feels disappointed and unhappy with her/his accomplishments over all those years, it means that the philosophy entertained by that person was not the best. However, since one cannot change the past, there is an option to transform it into a constructive and meaningful experience in the present. That is, we can peacefully accept our past as part of a grander picture, learn from it, and incorporate new ideas, thereby improving our chances for a positive, ever-improving, and fulfilling future.

Education is the major creator of any personal philosophy, and how we approach education today will determine our realistic expectations of tomorrow's human being. Through modern telecommunication and transportation accomplishments, the world is better connected than ever. Countries are closer together and different cultures are bridged in unprecedented ways. Education must follow suit: it needs to connect teaching disciplines by addressing their deepest meaning and interdependence. A complete education will enable people to select a better philosophy of life, which will bring success, happiness, and peace of mind. In the process, more inhumanities between people will be reduced or eliminated. Finally, by assuming an active responsibility to holistically preparing ourselves, instructors, parents, and students will ensure that the noble endeavor of teaching and learning will address mind, body, and spirit, in an honest effort to create a better future for all of us: complete education means real freedom.

2

The Passion of the Teacher

The smallest act of kindness is worth more than the greatest intention.

Kahlil Gibran

'Nobody can teach anybody anything' goes a saying, but one *can* create an atmosphere conducive to learning. Educators can develop ways of presenting information to make learning more accessible and enjoyable, especially with respect to secondary education and community colleges. One of the best ways to facilitate an open and constructive relationship with students is for instructors to demonstrate their love and passion for teaching. Nobody wants to attend a boring 'show.' Many inspirational stories suggest that each one of us is an individual who carries inside her/his unique life experiences. Years of academic preparation, together with events from our personal lives shape the way we teach. In the end, who we are we carry with us everywhere we go, including the classroom. The following stories and sayings capture this fact clearly and I encourage all of us to search for new ones in order to enhance teaching and learning.

* A man intended to move into this village, but since he didn't know anything about the new place he decided to visit with the local wise man. So, he asked the wise man: What kind of people live in this village? The wise man answered: I will tell you but first you tell me what kind of people lived in the village you are coming from? To this the man replied: Oh! They were all wonderful, great people to be with, they were very nice toward me! The same kind of people live in our village, answered the wise man. Not too much later, another man came to the same village and asked the same wise man

the same question: What kind of people live in your village? The wise man in response asked: What kind of people lived in the village you are coming from? To this the man answered: Oh, God! They were all mean people, very rude, and they treated me with disrespect! The same kind of people live in our village, answered calmly the wise man.

* It doesn't matter when, how, and where we squeeze an orange, out comes orange juice. Why? Because that is what is inside an orange. The same happens to us: when 'squeezed' by special circumstances and out come anger, impatience, and hate, it is because that is what we stored inside of us over time. The alternative is to pay more attention to what we put inside by our power of thinking, analyzing and selecting the experiences we allow to affect ourselves. This way we can store more joy, happiness, patience, good-will toward people (students), and in the end more passion for what we do. Consequently, when 'squeezed' by teaching and learning circumstances and out come patience, cooperation, love, and compassion, the results of our educational endeavor will be more positive, constructive, and long-lasting.

* If life hands you 'lemons,' you have the choice of making sweet and refreshing lemonade.

I hope we can all continue our search for better ways to deliver the teaching with which we have been entrusted, and that we chose as a profession. This book is meant to support this search. In the meantime we need to remember that teaching is one of the most important endeavors in the world, if not the most important. This motto on a coffee mug I received from a student summarizes it best:

"Those who can, teach. Those who cannot, go into a lesser line of work."

3

From Prison to Freedom

The truth is that our finest moments are most likely to occur when we are feeling deeply uncomfortable, unhappy, or unfulfilled. For it is only in such moments, propelled by our discomfort, that we are likely to step out of our ruts and start searching for different ways or truer answers.

M. Scott Peck

Imagine you are born in a room and you spend a number of years in that room only. That is all you know and all you could use to know the reality of the world in which you live. Information and all other necessities are given to you and you are not personally responsible for them. Also, the number of people with whom you interact is small and most likely close to you (relatives, friends, neighbors). Under these circumstances you have little impact on the world around you.

Then your world expands. You are released from that room and suddenly you realize that the house in which you live has a few more rooms alike or different from yours. Wow! You are taken by surprise as you are able now to expand your horizons, your experiences, and your perception of reality. Your level of responsibility increases once you find yourself in a larger world and so does your potential impact.

Then you get to leave the house you knew so far as your world. You realize that there is even more to the picture of your reality. You get to see many houses on your street, some alike, some different from your own. You interact with a larger number of people and consequently, you find yourself responsible for your actions at a higher level. Also, you realize that your impact on your new, expanded world increases in a variety of ways.

Teach For Life

Then you face an even greater reality: the street on which you live is not the only street in this town. Your world explodes into a multitude of intersections, stop-lights, stores, businesses, restaurants, and so on. Your understanding of the world changes again: your old limited reality starts losing importance. You have just jumped into a more fascinating and exciting life that implies greater personal impact and responsibility.

Then you get to leave your town. You visit several other cities in your country and you realize how much larger and captivating your new world is. You are starting to see that, in fact, you are a small but integral component of a nation that has its own specific characteristics. Within this picture you gain more wisdom and you become aware of your greater impact and responsibility in the larger scheme of things.

Author at the Berlin Wall, Germany, 2007

Then you get a chance to leave your country – or you decide to escape from a totalitarian regime that kept you isolated to 'protect' you from the 'wild' world outside. You get to visit many countries and more and more you realize the true wonders of the continent on which you lived. In the meantime, the old places, your house, street, town, and even your country make room now for an even greater reality that you finally get to experience first-hand, and you say once again: wow!

And that is not all. After a while you travel to another continent on your planet, perhaps overseas, and your horizon expands even further. Completely new ways of life come your way and you are amazed by the complexity of international relations, new languages you hear and learn, and new philosophies of life you encounter. You realize how profoundly traveling contributes to one's general education. Under these influences, intrigued, you change some of your old convictions developed over the years, as you find the new ones more logical and most importantly, more functional. With an open mind, your life takes a turn for the better with every step on your journey.

Your concepts of personal impact and responsibility expend even more, and you realize that you live on a planet that is in fact an impressively complex living organism. You finally can see yourself as what you really are: a vital and meaningful cell in this vibrant body called the world. As important as your formative years have been, all those places and cultural-religious experiences have lost their grip on you as you find yourself on the verge of the greatest realization of all.

And here it is: your planet is only one of several in your solar system. Your sun is only one of a myriad of them in your galaxy and your galaxy is only one in a virtually infinite number of galaxies in the universe. Within this scenario your planet appears as an infinitely small spec, a grain of sand if you wish, in the very largest scheme of things. It is, then, almost impossible to exclude the possibility of civilized life elsewhere in your cosmos, so your conclusion is that most likely the human race is not alone in the universe. And then you say once again: wow!

In your imaginary (for now) trip through the wonderful universe, you realize with awe that you and your planet are vital components within a perfectly orchestrated universal balance. You realize that what you have learned from your philosophical, religious, and quantum physics research are meant to support the reality of the universal energy that keeps the entire cosmos together, united in the most profound way. Against most of the "old" teachings, you can now get out in the street and shout loudly: WE ARE ALL ONE! You feel like embracing everybody as your own to tell them from the bottom of your heart: "Can't you see? We are all united!"

And then fantastic implications emerge. As you observe the entire human condition from the outside of your immediate reality (even in an imaginary way) you can better understand it. How can humans still inflict harm on other human beings? No, you cannot do that when you realize that we are all one, so hurting others in fact hurts ourselves. This is the true, and perhaps the most fundamental education we should receive and give: we are all one. Schools should teach it, parents should teach it, and religious organizations should finally adopt it to replace a philosophy of separation in senseless competition and discord. This conviction will really free us for a life open to all possibilities as we understand our true place in the universe.

Consequently, in unity, we can finally master a solution to all problems created by humans, including harm to our environment. This can be the real end of all worries and the beginning of a true happy era for humanity.

4

Teach Unity within Diversity

No tree is so foolish as to have its own branches fight among themselves.
Native American wisdom

In order to improve teaching, educators are constantly searching for new avenues to relate to students. Open communication enhances the chance for success in teaching and learning. However, the present educational paradigm is one of separation. Individuals are thought of as entities with no interconnection among themselves or the environment. This belief automatically implies an attitude of competition and discrimination which can often lead to hate and crime. Within such a paradigm we witness a myriad of negative acts between human beings, reality we cannot afford any longer.

Since most colleges teach students of different social and ethnic backgrounds, by adopting a unity paradigm, modern education can help people eliminate negative thoughts and discriminatory acts from their lives. In order to accomplish this goal, a shift in awareness must take place. The core of the unity paradigm is the conscious realization that each human being, regardless of sex, race, or religion, is actually an intricate element in a larger whole. Just by reason alone, then, we can agree that one person should never act against the well-being of another. To illustrate this, a metaphor comes to mind: since the well-being of a human body is implicitly dependent on each of its components, one hand does not intentionally stick a knife into other parts of the body; instead, it nurtures them, ultimately for its own good. This should also be the model for the relationship between people.

In the following I will illustrate how we can change our views of the world by exploring a variety of scientific and philosophical realms of human development. Support for such a change is provided by modern science (quantum mechanics, biology, etc.) and philosophy, hand in hand with some of the age-old wisdom.

The last century shows a convergence of such fields of study. They all agree that in our universe (uni-verse, one song) there is no physical entity that is completely separated from everything else. Indeed, at a subatomic level, each perceived individuality is part of a complex web of relationships which through their energetic nature create what we detect as physical matter. Carl Sagan, the late American astronomer, expressed the unity of the cosmos suggestively: if one atom could be removed from the universe, the entire universe would collapse. So great is the universal interconnection.

Stories that Can Change Lives

Many inspirational stories illustrate the reality around us and can help end dishonesty, hate, and crime by abolishing the old paradigm of separation in favor of an existential paradigm of union and interconnection. Moreover, discrimination based on gender, religion, or ethnicity is automatically banished. The benefit of this shift in awareness is monumental especially in the field of education, since it raises the level of personal responsibility in students, educators, and parents. Within the unity paradigm (awareness of the universal connection), injustice to others is a nonsense since all human beings are parts of the same whole called the Human Race. Moreover, by teaching values such as truth, respect, patience, compassion, and love, education becomes a more successful endeavor.

Who We Are We Carry with Us Everywhere We Go

Who you are shouts so loudly in my ears that I can't hear what you're saying.

Eastern wisdom

Teach Unity Within Diversity

If you work hard on your job, you can make a living. If you work hard on yourself, you can make a fortune.
Jim Rohn

How People Learn

Here is how a student from a weekend seminar in philosophy and self-growth described the human ascending walk through life, in five short chapters, on one page:

Chapter 1
I walk down the street. There is a huge hole in the sidewalk. I don't see it there. I fall in. It is not my fault. I have a hard time getting out. I continue my walk.

Chapter 2
I walk down the street. There is a huge hole in the sidewalk. *I see it there.* I still fall in. It is not my fault. I have a hard time getting out. I continue my walk.

Chapter 3
I walk down the street. There is a huge hole in the sidewalk. I see it there. I still fall in. *It is my fault.* I get out, I continue my walk.

Chapter 4
I walk down the street. There is a huge hole in the sidewalk. *I walk around it.*

Chapter 5
I walk down *another* street.

Anonymous

We Are All One - the Quest for Harmony and Unity in Diversity

Dr. Edgar Mitchell is the sixth person to have walked on the Moon. An obviously well prepared scientist, graduate of MIT, Dr. Mitchell took an active part in the NASA program, and in the early 1970's he earned the privilege to set foot on our natural satellite. He was admiring the quiet dance of cosmic constellations on the clear lunar sky, when suddenly a "blue quarter" appeared to his right. He was amazed to realize that the "blue quarter" (as he had named it later) was our planet, the Earth, which from the Moon resembled a blue coin of the size of a quarter. At that moment Dr. Mitchell experienced a 'satori,' as it is called in the East, namely a revelation: on that little distant 'blue quarter' one could find the entire history of the human race, with all the ups and downs from all times. On that 'quarter' were all the troubles and the happiness of our modern era, with the success and pain, with the riches and the hunger, and the aspirations and desolations of all human beings. With this picture in mind, Dr. Mitchell suddenly realized that the 'blue quarter' is just a small part in the whole scheme of the universal makeup, and it exists in a perfect cosmic order. The countless stars and galaxies visible from the Moon embrace our little 'quarter' in a perfect harmony, held in place by a mysterious energy. That energy is omnipresent, which implies that the entire sequence of events on Earth are also in perfect order and in perfect harmony with the rest of the universe regardless of our personal interpretation of the circumstances in which we find ourselves.

Back from the Moon, Dr. Mitchell left NASA and founded the Institute of Noetic Sciences (noetic - inner knowing). Its mission is to bridge the scientific and the spiritual avenues of human development in a quest for harmony and unity within diversity.

Sciences Underline Unity within Diversity - Some Examples

As diverse as the world around us is, more often than not its unity escapes us, or as the saying goes, we don't see the forest for the trees. We have seen how universal wisdom suggests the interconnection of all that is. Moreover, quantum mechanics, biology, and other fields of study support a similar view: at a subatomic level there is a continuous exchange of energy between any two seemingly isolated bodies regardless of the distance that apparently separates them. In his book, *The Turning Point*, Dr. F. Capra illustrates this very clearly. The two-hour video made after this book, entitled *Mindwalk*, is a vivid and entertaining representation of some of the quantum realities at work in the unseen subatomic realm.

The field of biology, through the work of Dr. Rupert Sheldrake, is also suggesting the reality of morphic fields of communication between remote populations of the same species. Many fascinating experiments stand at the foundation of his theory.

And finally, physicist David Bohm in *The Implicate Order*, maintains that there is no such thing as randomness. Instead, everything in the macro universe happens orderly, within the chain of cause and effect.

Consequently, based on all these considerations, we should support the implementation of the unity paradigm in general education. We teach by example and through our own efforts and behavior we should inspire students to adopt the philosophy of union instead of the present paradigm of separation and senseless competition and discord. Awareness of the interconnection of all that is in our diverse world will solve many, if not all of the existing pressing social problems, mainly by eliminating hate and crime at all levels.

5

Create a Meaningful Course Syllabus

To waken interest and kindle enthusiasm is the sure way to teach easily and successfully.
Tyron Edwards

In the following I will outline what I consider important and necessary in the process of creating a course syllabus. There is one common trend with respect to students reading all the information they receive at the beginning of a semester: many of them don't!

With this in mind I would like to start with a suggestion: the first class period of every semester should be almost entirely dedicated to a presentation based on the syllabus. After providing each student with a copy, instructors should guide their students through the entire content of the syllabus, pointing out what they consider the most important issues regarding the respective course of study. To ensure clarity and usefulness of the syllabus, instructors should not exaggerate its length, but they should not omit essential or required information.

1. The first part should contain "Instructor Information" such as name, teaching schedule, office hours and office location, phone numbers, email address, webpage (if applicable), as well as precise information on the respective course (name of the course, section number, course schedule, room number). All of this should be followed by a general statement addressing the importance of good communication between instructor and students and the usefulness of the course, both in the students' academic sequence and their life after graduation. Instructors should make an extra effort on reminding students that the

meaning of education, especially of higher education, is not only to learn the specific contents of the course, but also to improve personal skills that will last a lifetime. Such skills will really make the difference in their employment and their income. In the meantime, this reminder is meant to take some of the possible anxiety away by showing students the WHY of taking the course. Since I teach mathematics, I include here a statement regarding mathematics that I give to all my students at the beginning of every semester.

Welcome to our course in mathematics

"Assuming you are placed in the proper course, this one will definitely help you advance your academic preparation in mathematics. Moreover, I would like to mention a few other areas of lifelong benefits to you. In this respect, persistent study of mathematics will also enhance your personal skills as to: improve your <u>number sense</u>, develop a deeper sense of <u>personal responsibility</u> and <u>time management</u>, <u>concentrate</u> in order to perform complex tasks, become a better <u>independent thinker</u> (able to rely on yourself), <u>analyze materials</u> (sometimes even abstract concepts), <u>extract facts and follow details</u>, <u>draw logical conclusions, organize thoughts</u>, and <u>determine nonsense real life situations</u> such as no-solution problems or non-applicable solutions. Consequently, I hope you will approach this course with total dedication and joy in order to make it a lasting success."

2. The next part of the syllabus should explain clearly the testing-grading scheme. Instructors should explain their policy on tests, quizzes, homework, final exam, attendance, participation, tardiness, and absences. The way the final grade is determined should also be part of the discussion.

3. Most educational institutions require a standard departmental document that describes the course in details. Such information should definitely be included in the syllabus. This should contain the title of the textbook, the possible

additional supplements (software, solution manuals, etc.), information on the use of technology, and on the instructional methodology (lecture, computer mediated, distance learning, etc.). Issues concerning withdrawals, reinstatements, and incomplete grades are usually treated clearly in such documents.

4. One valuable page that I think should be part of the syllabus is a short list that summarizes advice given by the instructor's previous students to new students as to what will be a successful approach to the respective course. Every instructor can easily collect such comments from some of their classes to share with future students.

5. The course purpose, course description, and course requirements are important components of the syllabus in order to familiarize students with the course even before starting the material. This presentation should put things in perspective in terms of the place that course has in the student's academic progress toward graduation.

6. Every educational institution should have a clearly stated policy on: service to students with disabilities, scholastic dishonesty, student discipline, academic freedom, and course support services. Via the syllabus, students should be made aware of these policies from the first day of classes.

7. Last but not least, the syllabus should contain a detailed schedule for the course that points out the sections planned to be covered every week of the semester. This helps the instructor cover the material in a timely manner and assists the students in case of absences, test and review scheduling, and preparation for the midterm and final exams, if applicable.

I hope these suggestions help the creation of a meaningful syllabus that should optimize the teaching-learning experience. Instructors should adapt these ideas to their particular course of study and students should always pay close attention to the contents of the syllabus for a successful educational experience.

6

Self-assessment for Better Teaching

Most people search high and wide for the keys to success. If they only knew, the key to their dreams lies within.
George Washington Carver

It is common practice to rely on outside assessment in order to evaluate performance. Athletes compete against other athletes, art work is valued according to how others perceive it, and student progress is measured by educators in terms of grades, projects, participation, etc.

Regarding teacher evaluations, academic institutions resort to student evaluations, supervisor evaluations, and sometimes self-evaluations, which all consist of standard forms filled with standard questions. Depending on our experience, the set of professional values we hold is clear to us, except that in most cases it is the result of exterior feedback. Our answers to standard questions build a limited picture of our teaching effectiveness. On the other hand, self-evaluations conducted in a personal, investigative manner should bridge our outside and inside worlds, even though, they can make some of us uncomfortable. However, there is real value in personally assessing our own teaching performance.

This can be done in a variety of ways, some better than others, depending on how, when, and where we do it, and, of course, on the method we use. In the long run we can benefit greatly from self-assessment if we distance ourselves emotionally from our teaching process, such that we can view it from an objective perspective. Moreover, distancing ourselves even physically from the classroom can offer an even better picture of our teaching, examining it from the outside, as we will see shortly. Of course, we must accept the fact that the way we teach is not the only way and it might not be the best way either. Therefore, we should assess our teaching with an open mind and the willingness to change, adapt, and especially learn from this process.

How to Self-assess

One practical, easy to do, and cost-effective method is simply the use of a tape recorder in the classroom (these days digital ones are available also). It is quite an experience to listen to ourselves conduct a lecture. In the privacy of our offices or our living rooms, especially if we do it for the first time, the voice intonation, the jokes we make (if any), the questions we ask, and the way we ask the questions, the responses we get from our students, the hesitations, the tension, the emotions we show, etc., all can be perceived differently *after the fact*. Sensitive issues might become clearer when we listen over and over to the same particular audio segment. Such findings help us search for ways to enhance our performance and to avoid unnecessary negative or confusing situations.

Another method of actually *seeing* ourselves in action is obviously videotaping our classroom activity. This technique is being used with great results in most competitive sports and the reason is quite clear. The beauty of videotaping is that we don't only hear ourselves, but we also see our gestures, facial expressions, smiles, signs of impatience, anger, joy, love, compassion, etc. The classroom atmosphere comes alive on a videotape, offering a variety of clues to what we are doing well and what needs improvement.

The Larger Picture

Overall, these two self-assessing methods don't employ open comparison, competition, grading, or ranking, but they prove very valuable as chances to literally distance ourselves from the instruction process in which we are usually submerged with heart and soul. When we are given the possibility to view the larger picture of our performance and how that fits in teaching and learning, we can experience a revelation. The teaching-learning unity in the education process is evident when seen from the outside. In the end academic education has one of the most important implications in the development of human beings.

Consequently, the future of teaching and its social implications depend on our willingness as instructors to improve through constructive means. Self-evaluating by audio recording and/or videotaping our professional activities are two effective ways to keep us on this path.

7

The Use of Student Evaluations

Education is the ability to listen to almost anything without losing your temper or your self-confidence.
Robert Frost

In order to improve teaching we need to be aware of students' perception of our teaching. For this, institutions of higher education employ different procedures for students to officially evaluate their instructors. Some schools conduct such evaluations every semester, which I think is the best practice, and some do it only once per year. Of course the information that transpires at the end of these evaluations is especially valuable for instructors. However, since in most cases it takes place towards the end of the semester and the instructors do not learn the results until the beginning of the next semester they are not really useful during the semester in question.

In addition to this official evaluating procedure I suggest we use another one, less official, less time-consuming, and more personal. This is a short survey designed by ourselves as a brief questionnaire related to our individual field of teaching. The questions should be directed towards the issues that we as instructors consider important, but in the same time we should leave room for students to express themselves freely regarding aspects of the course in question. Most beneficial is the fact that this survey can be used any time during the semester, and consequently we can collect feedback from our students as the semester progresses. As a suggestion, I think we should conduct such informal surveys maybe every third of the semester. That will give us enough time to implement possible changes in our teaching during the semester in question, thereby providing means of adjusting to the respective class of students.

Another benefit has to do with anonymity. In most cases the official institutional student evaluations are anonymous, respecting student's confidentiality. However, as we understand this right I would like to suggest that at times we can implement informal evaluations where students do give out their names so that we can have a constructive discussion on meaningful issues. Such a practice will definitely increase the level of responsible involvement of students and will add to the value of the survey. Of course, a non-anonymous survey can only work after we have created a unthreatening classroom atmosphere where trustworthy and open-minded human beings (students and instructors) can express themselves without fear of egotistical repercussions. This way we can also enhance the level of communication and cooperation between us and the students, which in turn can take the teaching-learning endeavor to a higher standing.

Here are some suggestions on constructing a survey adapted to a particular course. The survey form should have a title and room for comments. We should give students four options on answering the questions: E (excellent), G (good), F (fair), I (improve). We should select anywhere from 10 to 15 questions or evaluative statements pertaining to our course such that we can learn about students' level of comfort in the class. The questions should be divided into two categories. The first should be concerned with students' perception of instructor's teaching approach such as: clearly stated expectations and objectives during each class period, clear and complete lectures, clear information on grading as the semester progresses, level of relaxation in class, respect for rules and for students, all meant to encourage an atmosphere of cooperation. The second should be concerned with students' perception of their own participation in the learning process such as: attendance, completing assignments, asking questions in class, using the available help offered by tutoring and computer labs, using the instructor's office hours, etc.

It should be left to everyone's choice of conducting anonymous or non-anonymous surveys, depending on preference, the nature of the course, and the respective group of students. Either way, the information collected should help both students and instructors improve the meaningful process of teaching and learning during that particular semester. The results can be amazing and most importantly, timely.

8

Grading: Learn to Love it

If you can find a path with no obstacles, it probably doesn't lead anywhere.
Frank A. Clark

As I converse with faculty around the country, it is evident to me that most of us, instructors, are not necessarily in love with grading papers which is perceived as a 'boring, time-consuming, tedious, and unpleasant' task. Since I consider myself a member of the minority on this issue, I argue that, we all need to learn to love grading. The main reason for this is that not only is grading an essential component of our profession, but we should also enjoy what we are doing, especially since our perception directly affects the outcome.

Indeed, all of us, teachers, instructors, and assistants find grading indispensable to the complex endeavor of teaching and learning. Therefore, besides pointing out its necessity and importance, I offer here a few other tips meant to help us love grading. In the meantime, every one of us should search for their own means to accomplish this worthwhile goal.

Do what You Love and Love what You Do

As we investigate closer what we do, we should realize that it is up to us, rational human beings, to choose the area of work in which we want to be involved. So, assuming that we do want to be in the teaching-learning profession, we should develop an appreciation for every single component of our activity in or outside the classroom. After all, it can be postulated that each one of us would opt for happiness in life which includes the time we devote to working.

However, one can argue that we should allow for at least some areas of less than perfect satisfaction and ease as teaching-learning is concerned. As a contra argument I would like to suggest that everything we know has been learned at one time or another. Therefore, since many of us definitely have learned to dislike grading - especially because we have been constantly bombarded with that message - we should find the energy to replace such a pattern of thinking with a more positive, constructive, and happier one.

When, Where, and How Fast We Grade

Since we are in general flexible as to when, where, and how fast we can grade, here are some ideas to happier grading:

1. We should grade our papers as soon as we can; I find it easier to grade them as they are turned in, as opposed to stacking them up for future attention. A quick turn-around not only benefits the students, but it will also help prevent overloading our future schedule.

2. We should grade where we feel more comfortable; in the office, at home (quietly or watching the news), or in the park. However, it is important not to grade when and where we are in an 'anti-grading' disposition; that is when we can reinforce a dislike for grading.

3. There are times when we grade at a slower pace. That is fine; we need to learn to enjoy taking our time as we recognize the importance of a job well done; besides, we don't have to grade an entire set of papers in one setting.

Other Ways to Start Loving Grading

First, my research shows that in many cases we exaggerate the amount of papers we collect from our students (too many tests, quizzes, homework sets, and exams); 'more' is not always equivalent to 'better.' By so doing we overload ourselves with unnecessary work, which can lead to a dislike of grading. Therefore, we should reconsider the number of papers we require students to turn in for grading.

Second, by using testing centers extensively, we don't experience the benefit of direct class time interaction with the 'test takers.' Conversely, giving tests in class whenever possible offers us a taste of the real testing atmosphere, gives us a chance to help the needy student if we find it appropriate, and it can also provide a little extra time for reflection and grading.

Third, we should view testing only as a tool used to identify what students do or do not know. We should be aware of the fact that the test grade is not a descriptor of a student's character, or of her/his overall ability to perform general intellectual tasks. Therefore, academic freedom should allow us to employ more often than not custom tests which permit partial credit, with room for positive feedback and correction. Grading should include our concern and care for the student's progress, which in turn will bring us closer to our students. Consequently, we can start viewing grading as a more sensitive and constructive activity.

Finally: Changing the Negative Perception on Grading

Since it is actually the second most important activity of instructors' professional life, we should consider grading as an open window to our students' learning and as a mirror for our teaching. The understanding of the subject matter and the level of comfort students experience in our classrooms often transpire from tests, quizzes, exams, or other papers. This realization should encourage us to examine our own efforts into the making of assignments and tests in terms of completeness, length, clarity, and difficulty. Therefore, the window and the mirror should merge for the benefit of the student.

Once we truly accept and understand the significance of these efforts, as teaching for success is concerned, we can easily change our perception on grading. Consequently, we will benefit from an optimistic, happy, and positive attitude about grading, which in turn will contribute to long-lasting professional fulfillment.

Author at his blackboard

9

Unorthodox Teaching of Mathematics

A teacher who can arouse a feeling for one single good action, for one single good poem, accomplishes more than he who fills our memory with rows and rows of natural objects, classified with name and form.
Johann Wolfgang von Goethe

Over all my years of teaching mathematics I have always emphasized the importance of understanding logically the concept in question. I always encourage students to ask what I consider the most important question of all: Why? In this respect I make sure students understand from day one that there are no 'stupid' questions; if one person has a question, that is a very valid question and many times it helps several other students who may have the same question but don't feel comfortable enough to ask. In many cases questions can be addressed to the entire group of students, as we, the instructors act as moderators. This approach opens up a free, guided, and mutually respectful cooperation in the classroom, which, in my opinion, makes the classroom teaching more productive, more complete as an educational endeavor, and more humane than any teaching and learning mediated by technology.

In the following I will describe such an example of a question that, at that time, made me and all the students feel totally stranded. The concept with which we were dealing was the rule of multiplication of signed numbers; in fact it all came down to why a negative times a negative is a positive? Or simply put, why the negative of a negative is a positive. I explained it as well as I have ever done, with examples and implementing 2-3 different known strategies, but one of the students sitting in the front row had a very hard time grasping the logic of it. The concern sounded something like this: "I'm sorry but it doesn't make sense to me." After exhausting all the time we had I promised that we will re-visit this concept next time with, hopefully, a better result.

As we all know, not all students think the same way and I had to remind myself that not all people are comfortable thinking numerically. That did it: I had to come up with something that did not include numbers, and I did. Next time I entered the classroom I ran to the blackboard and I started writing, engaging the respective student. "Let's name the sentence 'I go to school' P and let's write it like this:

$P = $ 'I go to school'."

Then I asked: "What is the negative or the opposite of this sentence and how would you write it?" The obvious answer was:

$- P = $ 'I don't go to school.'

Then I asked: "What will be the negative of the last sentence and how would you write it?" The answer came fast:

$-(- P) = $ 'I go to school.'

Then I asked: "Isn't this last sentence the same as the first?" To this, the student jumped up surprised and with great relief screamed out loud: "My God! $-(-P)$ is equal to P. I get it: a minus of a minus IS a plus!" Then I said: "Or a negative times a negative is a positive since 'of' in mathematics means 'times', isn't it?" The student responded in the most assuring way, convincing the entire classroom full of students and me that we have accomplished a great thing that day: "I get it. I finally get it. Thank you very much!"

Consequently, I want to encourage every one of us, instructors at any level to dig out meaningful explanations from our own experience, college years, and long 'forgotten' courses in logic, rather than solely from the course at hand. Mechanical learning might 'get the job done' for the time being but humans are not machines and I feel that we should bring as much logic and common sense as possible to all we teach. This does not only ensure a solid understanding of mathematical concepts but it also prepares the student for future situations in life when logic and rationality should prevail. After all, we *are* teaching for life.

10

Grading Homework in Mathematics?

Great ideas, it has been said, come into the world as gently as doves. Perhaps then, if we listen attentively, we shall hear amid the uproar of empires and nations, a faint flutter of wings, a gentle stirring of life and hope. Some will say that this hope lies in a nation; others in a man. I believe rather that it is awakened, revived, nourished by millions of solitary individuals whose deeds and works every day negate frontiers and the crudest implications of history. As a result, there shines forth fleetingly the ever-threatened truth that each and every man, on the foundation of his own suffering and joys, builds for all.

Albert Camus

In the following I will refer mainly to the teaching of mathematics but I think these ideas may also apply to other 'precise sciences' such as physics, chemistry, computer-science, finance, etc. Therefore, I encourage the readers to decide for themselves if and when they apply and to consider the consequences of adopting or ignoring such ideas.

Homework is an integral part of teaching since it is supposed to involve individual practice by students on the respective concepts. One main difference in how it is used in the process of teaching and learning is that some instructors grade it and some don't; some instructors give more credit for homework than others and some give none. With this in mind I propose an alternative to collecting and grading daily homework, based on the fact that students are unique human beings and they learn mathematics differently.

Issues

First I would like to analyze an intriguing reality I often encounter as I advise students in mathematics. Several times a semester I meet students who have actually failed other instructors' classes *only* because they did not turn in homework on time or at all; other than that they did well (A, B, or C) on tests and they even passed the comprehensive final exam. In other cases students passed a class with a minimum passing grade *only* because their homework grades were very high, but on tests, quizzes, and final exam they scored low. Now, what is wrong with this picture? The problem I see is that some instructors give, and in many cases give way too much credit for homework. Isn't the performance on tests, quizzes, and final exams a much better indication on students' mastering of the subject than their 'completion' of their homework? In this respect there are many situations when students can misuse homework by turning in work that does not really represent their true level of subject mastery, hence, the grade inflation. Here are two examples with suggestions.

Many students complain that they are doing their homework but they do poorly on tests and exams. To such a concern the answer is actually a question: how is the homework completed? Is there help from friends, classmates, family members, tutoring lab, solution key, or from the book and the notes themselves? This situation requires an extra effort of the student to work independently. Homework should be used by the student to simulate their test taking strategy. Therefore, independent thinking starts with 'work at home' or homework. After they understand the concepts, students should approach the homework practice set with as little outside help as possible, hopefully none. Only in extreme cases students should rely on help from other sources (tutoring lab, group work, instructor's office hours), and the classroom should be the next best opportunity to solve last-minute problems.

Here is a true story: a student responds to a friend when asked about the homework grade: "Oh! That is an easy 100. I copy it from my classmates or from the solution manual and turn it in." The remedy to such a problem is obvious.

Since students have different academic backgrounds and they might qualify under different kinds of intelligences, some do need more practice than others. Also, some need more practice on different concepts than others so we should not penalize them for not doing the complete set of recommended homework. Instead we should make sure students understand the importance of practice not only from the point of view of the respective course. They improve in many other areas as they assume the responsibility of working diligently on their homework: they learn to extract meaningful information, be better organized, learn to reason and estimate, get better on eliminating nonsense answers, and improve on selecting the best solution possible.

Moreover, one of the meanings of education is teaching personal responsibility in whatever endeavor we find ourselves. Instructors should encourage students to complete homework sets not for an immediate reward, but instead to view it as a long-term strategy to success. This is similar to the world of sports where athletes are rarely rewarded for practice. Rewards should come as a consequence of accomplishing a goal that can clearly be documented as the performance of the individual who is rewarded. In education this is realized by using well supervised quizzes, tests, and exams.

Strategies

Virtually all textbooks include at the back of the book the answers to the odd problems. Therefore, instructors can assign as homework only odd problems so that students can check their work themselves – this way students can 'never work in the dark,' they cannot say "I didn't know if I did this problem right or wrong." Simultaneously, students should be made aware of their paramount responsibility for their progress. Completion of their homework is an important tool in this respect so that *they* find out what they know and what they don't know.

Instructors can help this process in class. The first part of class activity should be spent on answering last-minute questions from the homework exercises, and these should be problems that were not clarified in the tutoring lab or with other outside help. This strategy offers the instructor the opportunity to review and, sometimes, re-teach concepts from the previous meeting, and to students a second chance to understand, or better understand the material. Moreover, students who were absent the previous class, have a chance to cover the concepts they missed. Instructors should never cover new material before students have a chance to ask *in class* questions on the previous concepts!

Next, once in a while (maybe once a week or once every two weeks), unannounced quizzes from the homework should be given in class. Such a quiz should consist of a carefully selected set of 2-3-4 problems, depending on the case, similar to the homework but not identical. In some cases notes and/or books can be allowed, and this should be at the instructor's discretion. These quizzes should be graded and their average should count as another major test grade. Students doing their homework consistently and independently should have good grades on quizzes, this way receiving their reward for their hard work.

Instructors should encourage students to save all their work (homework, quizzes, and tests) as they will eventually use them for final reviews and possibly in future courses. Instructors should include detailed information on all these strategies in the first-day-handout so that the students know from the start what is expected of them in the course. In this respect, the first meeting of every semester should be mostly dedicated to an open discussion and analysis of the general information included in the handout. Hopefully, good communication between instructors and students will increase the rate of success and students' comfort as they strive to complete their education for a better life.

11

Modern Education and Technology

Learning is weightless, a treasure you can always carry easily.
Chinese proverb

Over the ages human efforts have been mainly channeled toward making life easier, healthier, and more pleasant. Within this context, technological innovations have been made in order to reduce the brute force required to survive, to improve health, and to offer people a chance to enjoy their free time. However positive this intent may be, each innovation also carries risks and possible destructive implications.

The discovery that facilitated the avalanche of all the other 20th century technological marvels has been the electric current, and today we are dependent on it. The most essential tools, machinery, appliances, computers, telephones, stereos, and even toys function on electricity. The second half of the 20th century has been marked by impressive advances in electronics. The later decades of the last century witnessed the infiltration of computer technology into virtually every major area of modern life. From food preparation to entertainment, to educational software and satellites, computer technology has become indispensable. The manufacture and distribution of computer technology have become the fastest growing business opportunities of our time.

As computer availability increased tremendously, people began to appreciate the new technology especially for the speed of execution of preprogrammed tasks, for the capability of storing vast amounts of information, and for the world-wide access to such information. The initial use of networked computers was in the United States military. As time passed, this use was expanded into other areas, and today millions benefit from the opportunity to communicate with people all over the world by means of electronic mail. Due to the impressive storage capacity, electronic data banks make entire libraries available globally to business owners and interested researchers. Also the latest news is instantly available by a click of a computer mouse.

With all these facilities at our fingertips, it was only natural to employ computers in the realm of education. From their use in reading, writing, science, and mathematics classrooms, to "distance learning," computers have become an integral part of modern teaching and learning. However, a closer look at their role in some educational areas shows that this technology is in fact only a mechanical intermediary between teacher and student. In an era when real human values seem to be more and more neglected, it is obvious that employing an insensitive, electronic connection at the crossroads of teaching and learning might not always be a good idea. In his *Data Smog: Surviving the Information Glut*, David Shenk says it clearly under "The Laws of Data Smog:" "Computers are neither human nor humane" and "Putting a computer in every classroom is like putting an electric power plant in every home." Indeed, the classroom was primarily designed as a conveyer of *selected* knowledge within an atmosphere of debate and analysis, not as a facilitator of a flood of information.

Although for some people's personality a computerized intermediary might be recommended, from a psychological point of view it only serves to separate, or alienate, and to diminish the eye-to-eye human contact. The picture of a teaching computer lab often shows isolated individuals in front of insensitive machines. Some educators propose a departure from the classical "classroom lecture" style of teaching, favoring "computer mediated" teaching or even more, "distance learning." As we look closer at this picture we should ask some questions. First, within the computer mediated learning isn't it the computer actually lecturing to the student? Second, as a consequence, which kind of lecture should we prefer: a preprogrammed insensitive computer lecture or that from a sensitive human being as the instructor in the classroom?

Moreover, the extensive implementation of "cutting-edge" technology may appear to unite people by offering super fast means of communication. In fact, the opposite may be true. Under the illusion of talking to, or even seeing the other person on a screen, we are kept *physically* apart. The much praised accomplishment of virtual reality should be an important warning sign for the loss of appreciation of true *reality* as the world presents it to us. To experience a mountain climb while you are wired up on a seat in some movie theater, regardless of the felt authenticity of the electronically induced event, cannot substitute for the real experience of being on your own feet, smelling the unique alpine aromas in the pure air, as you feel your heartbeat propelling you through the grand scenery.

Therefore, we can already identify three major side effects of high-technology: (1) overwhelming and tempting availability of information, which for many is really not necessary, (2) physical separation between people, and (3) alienation from the true and wonderful natural realities of our world. The latter of the three raises another point of concern. Since new forms of high-tech entertainment have the capacity to create virtual excitement with little or no effort, more and more people are embracing such entertainment. Modern technology brings super realistic scenes to our eyes, ears, and minds on the large cinema screen, computers, or on the home television set. Violence in the news and in the entertainment realm has been condemned by many social and religious groups as detrimental to young and old. If we keep in mind the natural human inclination to experience excitement, we understand how high-tech creation of virtual realities can instigate the exploration of new possibilities for real, but often dangerous endeavors. From the sad reality of drug abuse and the danger of "extreme" sports (sky-diving, bunjie jumping, extreme skateboarding, etc.), to the technologically induced fear on occasions such as the extreme celebration of Halloween, recent years show a general tendency to push even the "fun" we desire to unsafe and often deadly levels.

Although there are many positive implications of high-technology, it can also be said that it facilitates manifestation of immoral behavior. In this respect, for example, the Internet opens up avenues for those inclined to pornography and pedophilia. In recent years, loss of privacy and stolen identities were also at the top of the list of negative use of technology. The FBI files speak volumes to this kind of abuse. More so, as we remember 9/11 and many other anti human acts, we should take notice of the use of high-tech in terrorist activities around the world. Also worth noting is the sad reality of full U.S. prisons in spite of all the recent advancement in technology; it is, therefore, obvious that such advancement does not take us to the moral and ethical behavior to which a civilized society should aspire in the 21st century.

Let us now consider the effects of the high processing speed offered by most electronic gadgets. In terms of obtaining information in a timely manner, such speed is to be appreciated; however, in many other areas of life it can have long-term detrimental effects. One negative long-term effect concerns our own health. From children to adults, as we compare today's life to that of some decades ago, we tend to rush more and more in everything we do. Whether going to school, or attending a soccer practice, or going to the movies, from a young age many of us live with the eyes on the clock. Educational institutions and practically every other source of teaching and learning seems to preach the same lesson: faster is better. Since "faster" seemingly saves time, we obviously ignore the quality of the experience for the sake of more experiential volume squeezed into the same 24-hour day. We see long lines of cars around unhealthy fast-food restaurants, we see people having breakfast or getting ready for work while driving, we see ourselves eating lunch while working, and then, by not paying attention to all of these realities, we act surprised by the high rate of heart problems, obesity, anxieties, addictions, and other long-term negative consequences.

One of the greatest human virtues that we sacrifice in our pursuit of this fast paced lifestyle is *patience*. As we strive to *do* and *be* more on our jobs, or at home, we lose patience. We don't have the time to patiently talk to a coworker, a friend, or even a member of our own family. We justify such behavior by pretending that being involved in more activities is really more important than building positive and sensitive human relationships. What is even worse is that, as adults, deeply submerged in this lifestyle, we actually teach it to our youth by example. We seem to forget the well-known saying: "the best thing you can give to your children is your time."

Saving time (and of course making money) has been the main motivation behind the mass production of a large variety of fancy electronic (often programmable) appliances, and we all know the multitude of time-saving gadgets present in modern homes. But the obvious question arises: what ever happened to the large amount of time saved by employing them? Indeed, it seems that we have less and less time for ourselves and our immediate families than our parents or grandparents had. Regarding the actual time spent working, it is worth noting that in some societies people used to have more holidays than working days in a year. As the world "evolves," the amount of time for celebration, rest, and appreciation of life is substantially decreased. This reality not only determines our actual vision of the world, but also dictates the way we understand our personal life.

After all these considerations we can see how a change in our perception on the use of technology is necessary in order to create a better future. In this respect I am proposing to all teachers, students, and parents a new model of well thought out inclusion of technology that is meant to help but not to make us dependent and addicted to it. This way, through a deeper understanding of who we are and what we are here for, as sensitive human beings, it will allow us to use safely and efficiently all the technological advances we treasure.

12

Education and International Olympiads

I am done with great things and big plans, great institutions and big success. I am for those tiny, invisible loving human forces that work from individual to individual, creeping through the crannies of the world like so many rootlets, or like the capillary oozing of water, which, if given time, will rend the hardest monuments of pride.
William James

<u>Olympiad Rankings in Mathematics</u>

In light of the 1997 and 2007 final ranking at the International Mathematics Olympiad (I.M.O.) some remarks are in order. Here are the first 10 countries and their scores in 1997:

1	China	223
2	Hungary	219
3	Iran	217
4	U.S.A.	202
5	Russia	202
6	Ukraine	195
7	Bulgaria	191
8	Romania	191
9	Australia	187
10	Vietnam	183

Now let us examine the situation in 2007 by listing the first 14 countries:

1	Russia	184
2	China	181
3	Vietnam	168
4	South Korea	168
5	U.S.A.	155
6	Ukraine	154
7	Japan	154
8	North Korea	151
9	Bulgaria	149
10	Taiwan	149
11	Romania	146
12	Iran	143
13	Hong Kong	143
14	Thailand	133

My first thought is related to the choice of selecting the 'top ten.' I would like to suggest that the first 10 places, and not 10 countries should be considered for statistical studies, and countries with the same score should be ranked equally. Therefore, for the 1997 I.M.O. U.S.A. and Russia should be both on 4th place and Bulgaria and Romania should be both on 6th place. Not only will this rank Russia and Romania on the accurate higher places, but it will also allow two other countries to be recognized within the first 10 places in the world.

My second remark is that out of the first 10 countries listed in 1997 only two (U.S.A. and Australia) offer their populations an acceptable standard of living in the world. None of the developed Western European nations such as Germany, England, Italy, Austria, France, Spain, Sweden, etc. made the top-ten list. However, the standard of living in those countries is highly comparable to that of the U.S.A. and Australia.

This brings me to my third remark: seven out of the first ten countries on the 1997 list either are, or have been under a communist regime. Relying on my Romanian background in mathematics education, I can say that the school system and the mathematics curriculum are designed differently in these countries compared to the U.S.A. The level of difficulty is pushed far beyond the U.S. median in secondary education. Moreover, a small group of students is selected and trained to achieve even higher levels of mathematics in order to successfully compete internationally (of course, the larger the population of a country, the better is the chance to recruit a talented team of "Olympians" - see U.S.A, Russia, and China). This is, however, an international approach as far as preparation for high-level competitions is concerned. But considering the difficulty (or the impossibility) of making a decent living in the free enterprise sector due to politics and high inflation, we witness the persistence of some very weak economies in parts of countries like Iran, Russia, Romania, Bulgaria, China, etc. Consequently, over several decades, those systems inevitably created low standards of living for many of their people, as compared to much of the Western world.

Over a ten-year span there is not much change. On the 2007 list of the first 14 countries we find only 3 or 4 where the standard of living is commendable (U.S.A.-5, Japan-7, Hong Kong-13, and perhaps South Korea-4). Countries such as Germany-15, Italy-21, Australia-22, Canada-27, United Kingdom-28, Sweden-41, Austria-42, France-43, Belgium-45, Switzerland-59, Denmark-65, and Spain-66 are not on the 'honor' list. However, the standard of living in all these countries, for the most part, is superior to many of the ones who did make the 'honor' roll.

As it appears, these become scenes of great contradictions. In many countries with a lower standard of living the math-science education (at least) seems to be used to produce a respected international image via international competitions. In the meantime, a solid academic preparation at both secondary and higher education level is achieved, but due to political reality and restricted economical freedom the standard of living for many is left behind.

The reality is, in fact, that in an overwhelming number of cases some of the best-educated students or professionals from such countries emigrate to the West where their high level expertise is much better rewarded. Unfortunately even today the respective governments do very little, if anything, to offer their own population a chance to a better future. In this respect it is well-known that in spite of a decent academic education, corruption continues to undermine any real progress for the benefit of all. We hope for things to improve as we move more and more toward a global economy and education in unity and cooperation.

Today's Mathematics Education in the U.S.

With this broad picture in mind let us now examine the teaching of general mathematics in the U.S.A. After all, it is well-known that math-science U.S. elementary and secondary students at large compare poorly to their peers from other developed nations, even if those countries don't make the top-ten list in international competitions. The question is: Why? On one hand, it seems that U.S. is one exception to the previous 'rule:' it is possible for a large country to prepare a solid Olympic team in mathematics and in the same time create opportunities for a satisfactory standard of living for its general population. On the other hand, after I have attended many conferences and professional meetings on math education, it seems to me that we in the U.S. witness a new and dangerous trend: U.S. students are progressively deprived of a solid foundation in elementary and secondary level mathematics due to a superficial and poorly planned curriculum, misdirected funding, lack of discipline and personal responsibility in the classroom, and incomplete teacher preparation. Most other countries do better in these respects by making sure that secondary education mathematics requirements go as far as Calculus and by offering a more detailed teacher education – they require a Master degree for teachers of secondary education in mathematics, including courses in philosophy and pedagogy.

In addition to poor preparation offered to U.S. high school students at large, in recent discussions on the teaching of developmental (remedial) mathematics at community colleges, there are suggestions to speed up this process by reducing the number of courses, creating fast-track courses, and/or watering down curriculum. How can one expect to remediate twelve years of everyday school mathematics (up to graduating from high school) in less than four semesters of biweekly developmental math courses?

Moreover, teaching to the test is another method practiced by some independent 'for profit' consulting firms, in order to show 'success' and to improve retention. In addition to this, the overly emphasized implementation of technology in the teaching of basic math skills deprives students of a real personal firsthand experience and understanding. All these approaches describe superficial and mechanical teaching of basic mathematics. Not only do these practices imply little success in college credit courses eventually, but they also create very limited options for students in their educational pursuits by failing to show the depth and beauty of mathematics.

As a result, at most U.S. colleges and universities, College Algebra, for example, which is one of the first college credit courses, is the course with the lowest success rate given the students' lack of basic skills and/or their faulty placement. In this respect, it is worth knowing that in many countries other than the U.S., undergraduate curriculum for College Algebra, Trigonometry, Precalculus, and Calculus I and II is incorporated into the secondary education: the 'high school' or Lyceum, or the Baccalaureate program of study.

Freedom without options is meaningless. This definitely applies to the teaching and learning of mathematics. Limited math education results in restricted options to students, as well as restricted versatility and limited growth potential. The modern world displays a great number of opportunities for people living in free countries, especially in this technological age when there is an imperative need for constantly updating one's skills. However, mediocre education produces mediocre graduates, which implies a modest effort to create a better society. Do we really want to support those educators and administrators who encourage speedy and therefore mediocre teaching of general mathematics in the U.S.? We shouldn't. Consequently, we need to reconsider the blind implementation of reform meant to cut costs and speed up the teaching of basic mathematics at both secondary level and two-year colleges.

Most of us mathematics instructors claim that we should teach excellence, which means to excel in the respective areas of study and practice. This surely excludes mediocrity resulting from watered down curriculum, fewer courses, and faster learning ('good things take time,' a song says). Are we displaying double standards within our activity as U.S. math educators? U.S.A. and Australia are on the top-ten list at the 1997 I.M.O. and they are the only representatives of the well-developed nations. Moreover, U.S. is also on the list of the first 14 countries in 2007. It shows, therefore, that through smart economics and a proper distribution of resources in education it is possible to ensure both a high standard of living and a notable presence at international competitions. But is there a majority of elementary and secondary education students under-served by asking too little of them in terms of their math-science readiness? As teachers of mathematics, let us continue to be for excellence in our important endeavor, and let us push for higher standards in elementary and secondary education so that U.S. mathematics becomes internationally competitive at *all* academic levels.

13

AACRAO's 'Official' View on International Education

The purpose of life is to increase the warm heart. Think of other people. Serve other people sincerely. No cheating.
The Dalai Lama

Although most of U.S. higher education is highly respected world-wide, we cannot say the same about U.S. secondary education. For many decades the U.S. math-science public secondary education has been stagnating at a pretty low-level and more recently it seems to be getting even worse. When compared to peers internationally, American students at large don't score very high. Public school systems from Europe and Asia seem to prepare students much better when it comes to math-science secondary education. This has been the subject of discussion many times over the years in the media and even at the U.S. Department of Education level but nothing has been done to improve the situation. At best, some officials proposed to throw more money at the problem in terms of more technology in the classroom, etc., forgetting that math and science education in most countries around the world is still approached with less emphasis on computers and calculators, and more practice and thinking meant to show the beauty and the usefulness of math and science at an elevated level of academic sophistication. In this respect, elsewhere, elementary mathematics, for example, is taught at a much higher level and more in-depth earlier than in the U.S. Consequently, in many other countries, students graduating from high school reach much higher levels of achievement than many of their U.S. counterparts. Although they graduate at about the same age, at the end of 12 years of school, high school graduates from the U.S. public education are at a disadvantage due to a less challenging and lower level slower paced curriculum in math and sciences. Reasons for this state of affairs have to do with misdirected funding, a possible arrogance, neglect, and rigidity on behalf of those representatives responsible for the integration of U.S. education in the international community, and the misevaluation of foreign education in the U.S.

Here is a concrete example on this theme. Since 2004 I have been researching practices employed by U.S. 'evaluation agencies' specialized in foreign academic transcripts. In this respect I focused on the evaluation of transcripts from Romania, since in 1979 I completed my higher education there (10 years before the 1989 Revolution), graduating from a 4-year institution of higher education with a Diploma de Licenta in Mathematics and Computer Science (Informatics). This was the last degree before a doctorate, in a two-step higher education system, but it was not called "Master." The Romanian Ministry of Education was able to set up such centralized programs of study in higher education due to the secondary school curriculum, the Baccalaureate. The Baccalaureate program, which was, and is, at a higher academic level than that of the standard U.S. high school, requires many undergraduate academic courses, which places the Baccalaureate program at the level of the second year of study in a traditional U.S. Bachelor program. (Please see Appendix 1: the entrance exam shows clearly what students must master before entering a Diploma de Licenta program in Romania). Since 1982 I have been teaching mathematics in Austin, Texas at both high school and undergraduate college levels. Based on my first-hand experience with both school systems, those of U.S. and Romania, I examined closely the practice of evaluating foreign academic transcripts in the U.S., and I have been completely disappointed by the rigidity and superficiality of the 'official' process.

One main organization engaged in this endeavor is AACRAO (American Association of College Registrars and Admission Officers), which is a self-appointed body whose governing board is composed of professionals from several

American institutions of higher education; on its own web-page it states: "AACRAO is a nonprofit, voluntary, professional association." In order to evaluate and integrate international degrees into the U.S. system, every 5 years, AACRAO sends committees to the respective countries to study and report on the possible recent changes in their systems of education. The committees return with recommendations that are published in brochures for each country, which are made available to for-profit 'evaluation agencies' all around the U.S. These agencies must be AACRAO 'accredited,' which simply means that their director must be an AACRAO member by paying a certain annual fee.

The Problem

Based on my extensive experience with the Romanian school system, I examined very closely the AACRAO brochure on Romania and my findings are staggering. It seems that the committee sent to Romania was mostly interested in the organization of the school system and not in the curriculum and, consequently, not in the academic level of the subjects of study. We all know though that in order to place foreign academic transcripts correctly into the U.S. system, one must examine the course work, the academic level, thesis written (if applicable), and not just the duration of study. A very unfair and hypocritical approach is that "one year of study in a foreign country is never considered more than a year of study in the U.S." In this respect, it is well-known that even in the U.S. students have the possibility to graduate early by taking overloads, by completing short semesters (12 weeks, 8 weeks, 5.5-week summer semesters, etc.), and even by challenging certain courses for full college credit. Moreover, the curriculum in other countries can be much more demanding early in elementary and secondary education, which will place the respective 'years of study' on a much higher academic level than in the U.S. Therefore, when evaluating foreign transcripts U.S. professionals should take into consideration a variety of details such as these, also including specific national, cultural, political, historical, and social aspects of the respective country. AACRAO does a very poor job at this and consequently, their "suggested placement" is often faulty.

A good example is the placement of the Baccalaureate Diploma (the secondary education degree) from Romania in the U.S. First of all, this diploma is very similar to the International Baccalaureate Diploma offered in some U.S. states as an alternative to the standard secondary education, for which, in Texas (per 2005 Texas legislation), students receive a minimum of 24 undergraduate hours toward their Bachelors degree. More than that, in pre-1989 Romania, the day of Saturday was a normal workday as well as schoolday from kindergarten through university studies. Consequently, the number of courses and implicitly the number of hours students completed were considerably larger than in the U.S. As mathematics is concerned, it is well-known that the Baccalaureate Diploma requires Calculus, which implies that at least College Algebra, Precalculus and Trigonometry (all undergraduate courses) are taken. It is also well-known that the standard high school graduation diploma in the U.S. requires as math credits only Algebra I, Geometry, and Algebra II. All courses beyond Algebra II are part of what is known as Advanced Placement (AP) courses for which students do earn undergraduate credits. Here is the big problem: in spite of all these facts, AACRAO evaluates the Baccalaureate Diploma from Romania only as the equivalent of a standard U.S. high school graduation, void of any undergraduate hours. Why? And this is not the only unjust evaluation (under-evaluating) imposed by AACRAO.

At the higher education level there is an even greater injustice. In Romania only students who earned the Baccalaureate Diploma can apply to universities or polytechnical institutes of higher education. In pre-1989 Romania students who would specialize in mathematics, informatics, physics, chemistry, biology, etc., for a university non-engineering degree, had to follow 4 years of very intensive study (6 days per week, 6-8 course hours per day), had to defend a graduation thesis in their specialization, and, upon graduation were employed as secondary education teachers, programmer-analysts, or researchers in their respective fields. The next step up, if they so desired, would have been at the doctoral level. Consequently, these requirements obviously situate the 4-year Diploma de Licenta from the pre-1989 Romania at the Master level as it compares to the U.S. higher education. In addition, as I carefully examined many actual U.S. Master transcripts in mathematics or mathematics education, it is obvious that the academic level of the Romanian Diploma de Licenta is very competitive and closely comparable to that of a U.S. Master degree. Relative to mathematics, a majority of the Diploma de Licenta courses are closely equivalent to U.S. graduate courses, and many professional educators of mathematics that I consulted with in the U.S. agree. In spite of all this evidence AACRAO evaluates the Diploma de Licenta from pre-1989 Romania only to a U.S. Bachelors degree! Moreover, 'evaluation agencies' do not employ professional educators as evaluators for each subject of study, especially at the higher education level, so they place foreign transcripts according to a rigid grid furnished by AACRAO's brochures. WHY? In this respect, I wonder how many transcripts from other countries are being similarly under-evaluated by AACRAO! How many thousands of students and graduates from around the world are set back this way financially and professionally as they immigrate to the U.S., actually being robbed by an unfair and illogical ad-hoc system with a possible agenda? Or is it all just a case of incompetent performance?

Possible Explanations

During my extensive inquiry I have been offered a variety of reasons for this obvious under-evaluating rigidly imposed by AACRAO. Some of the 'explanations' come straight from AACRAO's present or past presidents or vice-presidents. Moreover, one staff member from such an 'evaluation agency' confessed confidentially to me that they have numerous clashes with their own 'director' who is pressing them to under-evaluate many foreign transcripts, even when it is obvious that those graduates should receive a higher placement (evaluation) according to their course of study. At least one such graduate from a South-American country took this particular agency to court.

Within my research I expressed my concern that students and/or graduates from other countries (Romania in particular) are set back when they come to the U.S. One AACRAO ex-vice-president expressed it this way: "American students are also held back when they study in Europe." This sounds like a pay-back, as well as an unjustified pay-back. It is unjustified because the reason some American students are perhaps held back when they study in Europe is because of the academic level differences (discussed above) between the U.S. public high school courses and those of Europe. Such under-evaluating should not be practiced on any pay-back basis in the U.S. since most students and graduates from European schools are well prepared in math and science, and they work hard to continue their studies and rebuild their lives in the U.S.

A second reason for this under-evaluating and discriminating invoked by the same AACRAO ex-vice-president was that, even though in pre-1989 Romania there were 6 working days a week, with 6-8 daily hours, in the U.S. system "students have homework," ... as if in Romania there was none. This is totally absurd and shows a lack of information on behalf of AACRAO. I can testify based on my own experience that there *was* daily homework at all levels of study in Romania, including higher education. Moreover, in each course of study, the lecture was paired with a seminar meant to deal with homework, applications, and in-depth analysis of the respective course-work; also, in higher education, no courses or seminars were taught by graduate students, as is the case in the U.S. Due to this solid program at least in math-science majors, the Romanian presence on the international stage was and is a remarkable one – most Romanian students and/or graduates do well in other countries.

A third reason cited by an AACRAO director to justify the under-evaluating practice at all levels was that the International

Baccalaureate is not commonly recognized in the U.S. I would like to suggest that as long as it is recognized in a few states, and since the U.S. enjoys such a decentralized educational system of higher education, the similar Baccalaureate Diploma from other countries (Romania) should be evaluated at a much higher level than the basic U.S. high school diploma. The Romanian Baccalaureate Diploma should earn those graduates at least 24 undergraduate hours, which will place the 4-year Diploma de Licenta mentioned above to the level of a Master degree from a U.S. institution of higher education.

Also, U.S. Master degrees from different universities in a specific field are not 100% equivalent to each other due exactly to the decentralized nature of the U.S. education system. In this respect, the course content, number of hours, thesis (or no thesis!), and other requirements are in many cases significantly different at different institutions. A Master degree in mathematics from Texas State University, for example, is not identical in requirements to one from UCLA, or Ohio State University. Consequently, based on this, it is hypocritical for AACRAO to under-evaluate foreign transcripts.

Another disturbing reality that might explain this under-evaluating practice of AACRAO, is the fact that the U.S. business, financial, and educational organizations favored by AACRAO in the evaluations, are actually the customers of AACRAO. Many such customers express gratitude for the evaluations provided since they are, of course, content with the under-evaluation of their future employees and/or students who have just arrived into the U.S.A. The reasons are obviously financial: businesses may compensate the new employees less, since they are evaluated lower than what their qualifications show at closer scrutiny. Similarly, under-evaluated foreign students, when they are admitted to American educational institutions, will have to take more courses they don't need, which enhances the institutions' revenues (international students pay considerably more in tuition than other students). Sadly, most international candidates for such under-evaluations, new to the U.S. and not fully understanding the U.S. educational system, accept the under-evaluations, setting themselves up for big and irrevocable financial losses for years to come.

Conclusions and Suggestions

With all this said, it seems very difficult to believe that the U.S. secondary education will become internationally competitive any time soon as long as the system maintains the arrogant attitude of false superiority imposed by organizations such as AACRAO. Ignoring developments elsewhere, not recognizing the true value of other educational systems, and even worse, under-evaluating the academic preparation of international students and graduates, stops the innovation and prevents the adoption of better approaches in the U.S. math-science education. The AACRAO practice of under-evaluating foreign transcripts implicitly forces international students or graduates to take courses and earn U.S. degrees that they don't need - is this a clever way to extort money from generally poor people who can barely survive their first years in a new country as they also have to learn or improve their English? Instead of benefiting from "new blood" the present U.S. system creates more of the same by altering those candidates' academic preparation. Oddly enough, as a curiosity, the coach of the pretty successful U.S. Mathematics Olympiad team has been for many years a well-known Romanian mathematician.

Consequently, I would like to suggest a drastic change in attitude and practice towards the evaluation and placement of foreign transcripts into the U.S. system of education. Everywhere in the world degrees are earned by completing academic programs where course curriculum and research projects may vary in length and depth from country to country and even from institution to institution. Those are the areas that must be scrutinized when evaluating international transcripts. Unfortunately this is what AACRAO is not doing; evaluation agencies under AACRAO must employ experienced mathematics educators to evaluate math transcripts, physics educators to evaluate physics transcripts, and so on. It is imperative for AACRAO to focus on curriculum, academic level of courses, and the research thesis required by a certain higher education degree, all of which AACRAO is not doing. To be "fair and accurate" as they claim, AACRAO will fulfill much better its self-proclaimed 'mission' by spending its resources on directly comparing the international curriculum course-by-course to that of the U.S., instead of evaluating foreign transcripts based *only* on "duration of study." As I already presented, 4 years of a Baccalaureate program as secondary education is much more than the 4 years of a traditional U.S. high school, and it must be recognized as such. Moreover, 4 years of 6-day weeks university studies that followed the Baccalaureate program in a country like the pre-1989 Romania, is much more than just a U.S. Bachelor degree and it should be recognized as such, namely a Master degree.

In light of all the arguments presented here I hope for a constructive change implemented in the U.S. evaluation of international academic education. If AACRAO is not capable of evaluating foreign transcripts accurately, it should give up this role and let academic institutions employ their own professionals to accomplish this delicate task at an individual level for each subject of study. Until AACRAO reexamines and amends its procedures on evaluating foreign transcripts I encourage all international candidates for such evaluation to question AACRAO directly whenever an injustice is obvious. The evaluation of international transcripts plays an important role in the integration of those candidates into the U.S. and, if done right, many students and graduates from other countries will bring their truly valuable contribution to the substantial improvement of the U.S. education system at all levels.

14

Religion and Spirituality in Modern Education

A teacher's job is to bring to life mind and spirit, to give you courage to live a whole life. They have precious little time to do this in the modern school but, with astonishing frequency, they succeed in doing it anyway.

Bill Holm

The general trend is to keep religion and spirituality outside of the realm of general education, and this is done for several reasons, among which is the important 'separation of church and state.' It is recognized that our Constitution prohibits any government or governmental agency from establishing, or prohibiting any particular religion. However, as soon as we open a dollar bill we read "In God we trust." It seems to be a contradiction to exclude natural order or spirituality from general education especially in these days, when even sciences (quantum physics) take education ever closer to the natural order or spiritual philosophy of the East. The most recent picture of the universe is not of a machine running out of steam, but it is simply the physical manifestation of a natural or higher intelligent order, call it God or the Universal Intelligence, natural intelligence, natural order, omnipresent, omniscient, and omnipotent. This order keeps the universe together within a perfect balance based on universal interconnection and interdependence; the late physicist and astronomer Carl Sagan put it best: if one atom could be removed from the universe, the whole universe would collapse. This implicitly means that the higher order is everywhere, including the human beings, and consequently, any respectful educational system should make natural order part of its endeavors. In this respect, Carl Sagan also suggested that we are the awareness of the universe!

How else could we think about and debate the meaning of life and our place in the larger scheme of the universe?

Author at the Balea Waterfall, Romania

The argument "I don't subscribe to any religion, I am an atheist" should not subvert or destroy our quest to understand the universe. Not believing in a personal, cruel, and revengeful God could be one's choice, but not being aware of the order or intelligence that sustains the universe, including human beings (cell by cell, I might say), should not derail our search for all facts. We might not want to call this belief "religion" but it is a belief never the less. Even more, the natural order or universal intelligence (Universal Order) is now supported by science, which helps, at a deeper level, to fulfill our duty to obtain the scientific facts, and, thereby further our understanding of our universe.

There is a great distinction to be made here: a religious person believes in God, while a spiritual person is open to obtain the facts. I suggest an understanding of that energy that keeps the entire universe together and permeates every cell with order or intelligence. As we examine the human body, it is evident that even from conception the undifferentiated cells know what they will become eventually: some will divide themselves to become the bones, some to become the skin, some to become the brain, the heart, the kidneys, etc. How do they know if not by some natural or intelligent message that comes to them or is built into them ever since birth? This is a logical explanation of one of the greatest mysteries of life.

In this respect, modern education should strive to explain why things work the way they do and not just how they work. The model of an insensitive, mechanical universe appears to be less likely correct, now that we have a much better understanding of the world of subatomic particles that, alternately, also manifest themselves as waves, depending on the method of observation! With this model in mind it is not reasonable anymore to keep natural order or spirituality away from education at large since this explanation is supported by modern physics, and by recent discoveries based on experiments in mind-body medicine such as the placebo effect.

Consequently, we, the educators of the modern era should strive for a balance: as we teach the nuts and bolts of any academic discipline, we should also be prepared to introduce solid elements of natural order, spirituality, and universal interconnection and interdependence to which we all belong. To use only the teaching of current science or the already established religions, sociology, government, history (his-story!), and the specialized disciplines meant to prepare functional adults, is to risk a future that may lack depth, meaning, purpose, and progress toward a well lived life! It follows logically then, that over teacher-education, or soon after, educators should be prepared to offer their students a complete picture of what human life in the interconnected world means.

My own experience in this realm is a good example of the effectiveness of such teaching. While teaching mathematics I always include short elements of natural order or metaphysics, of course as they connect to mathematical concepts such as systems of equations, for example; it is impressive to notice how receptive students are to practical and applicable ideas that attempt to explain aspects of our lives not currently explainable by science alone! It is amazing to know how many students have had unexplainable experiences. Moreover, it is well-known that basic practices of deep breathing, relaxation, and brief meditation can help students reduce or eliminate anxiety while taking quizzes, tests, and final exams, which translates into better academic outcomes.

Therefore, new millennium teacher preparation at all academic levels, should definitely include natural order or holistic training to move toward a complete understanding of the meaning of life, and most importantly, to try to answer questions like "Who are we," "Why are we here," and "Where are we heading?" In the meantime, regardless of the subject of study, students should be the first ones to ask existential questions. Even if they don't, educators should offer tentative answers or encouragement for perpetual analysis of such hypothetical questions in order to trigger deeper thinking about life, as Einstein so powerfully stated: "The life of the individual has meaning only insofar as it aids in making the life of every living thing nobler and more beautiful. Life is sacred, that is to say, it is the supreme value, to which all other values are subordinate."

15

Save Handwriting!

The classroom should be an entrance into the world, not an escape from it.
John Ciar

As we all know, handwriting is becoming more and more a thing of the past for obvious reasons, availability of printing technology being the main one. However, I would like to argue that by accepting this trend we will deprive ourselves eventually of one of the most personal commodities that describes who a person is, how a person thinks, how organized a person is, and other important traits of a psychological nature.

There have been many studies on handwriting published over the years and in some cases handwriting has been used even to pick and/or qualify jurors and to solve crimes. All these point to the personal nature of handwriting and how it can be used as an accurate mirror of the personality and character of the respective individual.

For many of us gone are the days of letters written by hand. Instead, we type emails, we text-message, we even send typed letters to friends or family members, and we type job applications. In many cases educational institutions don't accept any but typed assays and even more, faculty members are constrained by some invisible force of conformity to type as much as possible.

Instructors of mathematics, especially, still can take advantage of their handwriting skills since most of the teaching is done on the blackboard or marker-board. Over the many years of teaching mathematics I found that handwriting is one major uniting practice between instructor and students since the students also take notes in class and complete assignments, quizzes, and tests in their own handwriting. By the fact that the instructors write by hand on the board and grade students' work by hand possible barriers in communication can be avoided. This way, instructors can be perceived as less threatening individuals by their students, which implicitly facilitates the learning process. If we include here the flexibility offered by handwriting on board or on paper in terms of erasing, correcting, completing previous work, writing foot-notes, and also working indoors or outdoors, we can see how handwriting should still be a treasure worth saving.

From the perspective of a long-term math teacher that I am, I can say that math instructors can also save an incredible amount of time (handwriting tests, quizzes, and exams) by not having to type all the text and especially the multitude of mathematical formulas, regardless of the software available. Can you imagine how we can use the time freed this way? One can find more educational books to read, videos and movies to watch, and, why not, constructive hobbies to entertain.

Other important "features" and benefits of handwriting tests and exams are the security involved and the comfort level of the students. In my case, every new semester I write completely new ones due to the easiness of handwriting; this allows me to give back tests and even final exams to students for further correction and learning without the 'fear' of insecurity since I will not use the same tests the next semester. Moreover, since most of the teaching takes place in handwriting on the board, via over-head projectors, or on paper as in grading, the students are always familiar with the handwriting of their instructors and, personally, I have never received student complaints or requests to type up the tests or exams.

Examining this issue from the point of view of "academic freedom" I am all for the freedom of choice that each instructor should enjoy. Some say "if it's not broke don't fix it," so I think this is definitely the case: there is absolutely nothing wrong with using handwriting in academic endeavors wherever applicable.

In the end, besides eye-to-eye communication, using handwriting can be the one best way to save some of what is

Save Handwriting!

left from us being human versus becoming completely computerized, programmed, and printed into universal shapes that ignore who we really are. The personality and the character of a human being come alive as we handwrite and they are not as evident when we print. The individuality of every person makes our world of diversity so fascinating today, as opposed to the uniformity and conformity to mechanical, artificial, unnecessary technological standards some try to impose in their pursuit for higher profits. If we pair this to so many cases of lost identities facilitated by technological means in the modern society we can say again and again: save handwriting!

16

Humor in Teaching and Learning

The thousand mysteries around us would not trouble but interest us, if only we had cheerful, healthy hearts.
Friedrich Wilhelm Nietzsche

Most good speakers start their presentations with a joke or a light and humorous story in order to ease possible tension and anxiety in the audience. The same should apply to our classroom teaching. After all, regardless of the pedagogical approach, we are making presentations every time we step in front of a group of students. One can always convey information easier within a relaxed atmosphere, and this applies as much to the presenter as it does to the audience, our students.

Who ever wants to attend a boring show? By this I mean that one successful way to engage an audience is by ensuring a light enough atmosphere such that individuals are sufficiently relaxed in order to concentrate on the subject at hand and to express themselves. So many times I have received comments from my students as they explain to me how uninteresting and boring some other classes were. The main complaint being about the attitude of many instructors that reflects rigidity and an imposed distance between themselves and the students, it seems logical that they, the instructors, must change their approach to teaching and consequently, the class atmosphere. Of course some subjects of study are more interesting than others to some students, but that is not an excuse to prevent instructors from creating a classroom environment suitable to learning and, even more importantly, from bringing lightness and flexibility to the process of teaching.

In this respect, sources of inspiration are multiple. From TV shows to the newspapers, and from personal anecdotes to those related by some students, there is a great volume of relevant stories for the classroom. Of course one must guard against offensive subjects, searching for "material" proper for an academic institution, and at the same time educational, at least to some degree. It is also understood that such use of classroom time should be minimal and timely: there can be many "dead" moments in a lecture/presentation when bringing in a tasteful story can be a good rescue. Sometimes very simple apparently meaningless nonlinear jokes can do a good job. Some years ago a student gave me as a gift a little – very little – book, entitled "Bad Jokes." Here is a sample: "What did the frog say to the elephant? …. Nothing! They don't talk!" Recently another student shared a "math" joke with me. Here it is: "We will never run out of math teachers. Why? …. Because they always multiply!"

In general students appreciate a good sense of humor but I do not mean to imply that instructors should play the role of a clown in the classroom – that can be detrimental to the teaching/learning process. Not everybody has the same inclination when it comes to humor, but we can all improve in this respect in order, first of all, to lighten up in our own lives, and then to bring some level of lightness in our interaction with the people around us, especially our students. After all, who we are, we take with us everywhere we go! Since we devote such a large amount of time to our teaching, it follows logically that we should strive to create the best classroom atmosphere at all times in order to eliminate anxiety, fear, and eventually burning out. The alternative is that these sensations can definitely affect the quality of our professional efforts and that will do a great de-service to our students, whose lives we affect every day of the semester.

Consequently, it is the instructor's responsibility and/or choice to conduct optimal activities in the classroom such that in the end students and instructor alike will have a pleasant experience. A nice and relaxed classroom atmosphere not only helps the education process and the relationship between instructors and students but it will also remain as a positive memory for all involved. Moreover, through word of mouth, future students will be attracted to instructors who truly enjoy what they do and, more importantly, who show it in the classroom.

17

Discouraging Lecture?

Teaching is the essential profession – the one that makes all other professions possible.
David Haselkorn

There is a trend in modern education to encourage a departure from the "old" teaching methodology of lecturing in favor of a variety of 'new' approaches. For a start I would like to list a few popular new ones: teaching in groups of students (self discovery), mediated learning (guided use of software), and distance learning (exclusive use of computers).

An often-used expression to describe this trend is: "Don't be a sage on the stage, be a guide on the side." Even in the literature outlining certain educational conferences or workshops it is suggested to presenters that "The traditional lecture format is discouraged." I think it is way too drastic and even counterproductive to drop lecturing in favor of other approaches, and I will explain why.

First of all it is pointless to constantly "reinvent the wheel," as a saying goes. In mathematics for example, asking students to invent and/or discover for themselves (by themselves) basic concepts that have been known for hundreds or thousands of years, often takes much longer than if those concepts are intelligently presented by a professional educator. A lot of frustration can be eliminated by an instructor who introduces new concepts with proofs and reasons followed by meaningful examples and applications. It is true that many times in life we learn by experience what to do and what not to do. However, to implement this kind of learning exclusively or even extensively in education is not the best practice. After all, the fundamental way we learn is by being exposed to the concepts we need to learn, *to be told* (lectured to, if you want) what works and what doesn't. During our life experiences we are actually *told* by the respective results what works and what doesn't. We then, hopefully follow through with what works and keep going. So, the bottom line is that *even* by experience we are somehow *told*, or, if you prefer, we are somehow *lectured to* by the situation we place ourselves in, and that is how we learn.

Group Learning

Similarly, when students try to learn (discover) in groups invariably one or more students in those groups assume the role of the conveyers of information. They provide explanations, reasons, and procedures for the rest of the group by, in fact, *lecturing* to them! Especially in sciences, where reasons must be provided, pedagogically untrained students often teach others most of the time mechanically (how to). Then, there is a problem with taking good notes which is definitely hindered in "group work." In this respect, for a thorough understanding of new concepts and procedures the question "why" should be the one to accompany explanations instead of only the question "how." Moreover, during such "group work," where the qualified instructors are "guides on the side," they only seldom use their high-level expertise on the subject. This really deprives students of the best explanation available in the classroom, the "sages" wasting their talent "on the side." After all, if you would attend a presentation by a famed mathematician wouldn't you prefer to hear that person present instead of "working in groups?" We, as instructors, *are* those famed presenters in the eyes of our students.

Therefore, I think the students are much better served by being *lectured to* by a professional who can also guide them through the individual practice necessary to assimilate the respective concepts. Of course the instructor should be able to create a classroom atmosphere where students *are* engaged, *are* participating, and *are* communicating their level of understanding. In this respect instructors should remind students of their own responsibility in the process of learning. Taking charge of their own progress is a trait they will treasure everywhere they go.

Mediated and Distance Learning

Considering mediated and distance learning we should praise the values that new technology can bring to modern education, but simultaneously we should be aware of possible downfalls. In this respect, making use of technology (computer software, email, etc.) can offer a chance for education of students at remote locations or students who, for solid reasons, cannot attend a course in a classroom. At the same time, the previous considerations are valid again. While a student learns by the use of a computer, we should notice that the student is *lectured to* by the software! In mediated learning, yes, there is an instructor present to help students in the computer lab, but most of the learning takes place on the screen of the computer. As a parallel, in distance learning even the physical presence of an instructor is absent. Not only does it become more difficult for students to learn and *understand* (software mostly teaches the "how" and not the "why") but they are also isolated from other human beings – the success rate in such courses is significantly lower than in the classroom set up. The precious human contact is virtually lost on the altar of "modern" teaching.

Based on my own experience I can underline how important physical interaction between instructor and students in the classroom is. Countless times simply *looking* in the eyes of my students I detect understanding or confusion. *Immediately* I step in to help with whatever problems there might be and only then move on. Thus, the open communication between students and instructor and between students among themselves is the fabric of good teaching and learning – we, humans, are social beings after all. We need to remember that instructors also learn in this process and, most importantly, we don't teach *only* the subject matter in the classroom. By whom we are and how we conduct ourselves, both instructors and students, teach and learn much more from each other. Responsibility, patience, cooperation, tolerance, humility, compassion, and love are traits that enhance our lives tremendously, but they are best nourished *in person* with human to human interaction. These traits are almost completely neglected as long as the process of education is mediated by insensitive technology. That is why we should strive for a well-intended balance in education such that we don't miss out with respect to human contact in favor of exclusive use of technology.

Therefore, we should not abandon *lecture* just because some want to cut costs; as with many other educational issues, they might be very wrong (see the "reformed calculus" efforts of some years ago). Moreover, we need to realize that the trend to move away from lecture is also motivated by a huge financial gain for all those who produce and market technology. Pairing this with an inherent human inclination to try-out and play with new gadgets, we put ourselves in a situation where we can sacrifice very valuable human qualities on the altar of technology. After all, it is obvious that modern life, in this technological era, may not offer higher moral and ethical standards compared to the pre-high-tech period. A quick look around the world allows us to say that such standards went progressively down as we "evolved" technologically.

Consequently, I suggest that all of us involved in modern education, teachers, students, and parents, think twice as we try to incorporate any "new" approaches into the process of teaching and learning. Change just for the sake of change is often a disaster. Lecture in all its forms is the *only* way we learn: an experience lectures to us, software lectures to us, a TV screen lectures to us, the books we read lecture to us, so why not treasure and enjoy a good lecture prepared and conducted by a professional educator? What's wrong with that? After all, most if not all of us have received our education through classical lectures of many types and we all remember at least some fantastic professors who have really captured our attention and interest with their unique style and well-organized *lectures*. Some of the most moving educational experiences I have ever had have been furnished by talented human beings "live" in front of very engaged audiences. Therefore, I hope we can preserve what is truly valuable from the "old" as we *cautiously* adopt the "new" in modern education.

18

Learning by Memorization

You gain strength, courage, and confidence by every experience in which you really stop to look fear in the face... You must do the thing you think you cannot do.
Eleanor Roosevelt

GOHUGEASLABULUNGPECUTA

I was in 5th or 6th grade when in a history class we had to learn about the ten most important migrating tribes, in chronological order, who passed over the territory of Romania before year 1000 AD. After a lengthy presentation, at the end of class, realizing how much anxiety all of us, students were under, the teacher offered to make our lives a little easier and wrote on the blackboard: GO-HU-GE-A-SLA-BUL-UNG-PE-CU-TA. While leaving he said: "Memorize this word and you will know them all." I think he should have said that we will know them for life, which is definitely the case as far as I am concerned. It is true, though, that I 'practice' a little every year by mentioning this story in my own classrooms, but under any circumstance, it is a 'word' that one cannot forget quickly – after all, we remember easier the out of the ordinary as opposed to the mundane.

So, my point is that memorization is actually at the foundation of all learning and it should not be discouraged; a systematic use of memorization can actually make many educational tasks much easier. However, in today's educational circles especially, I hear more and more professionals encouraging a variety of learning strategies, such as 'learning by discovery,' ignoring the fact that in the end we retain by memorization even what we discover ourselves. Yes, initially we should be presented with the "why" 5 times 7 is 35, but in the end we use this information simply by memory, and the same happens in most practical areas of our lives. It is essential to understand the "why" of all we learn, but this should not diminish the relevance of what we really know by memorization and we should not forget that the human brain has an immense storing capacity.

In mathematics, more so than in many other disciplines, it is imperiously important to develop a good memory as we have to recall a large number of formulas, theorems, patterns, properties, and procedures. Knowing by heart a majority of trigonometric identities, for example, simplifies solving equations, graphing, and solving application problems involving trigonometry. Also a good number sense usually translates into a well-organized thinking pattern that can make a difference in one's life. In this respect we have to agree that our number sense is acquired largely by memorization and persistent practice can reach notable levels of expertise.

Consequences

Since the human brain's ability to store information is much more impressive than it is thought, the more meaningful data we can access by memorization the easier it is to use it. It is not only that the level of personal satisfaction rises when we are able to complete certain tasks quickly, but also the productivity in the line of work or in life in general increases. In addition, we should not forget the health benefits an active and sharp mind can bring, which includes memorization. The medical establishment has made this fact clear repeatedly over the years, especially for the elderly. Therefore, we should view 'memorization' as a treasure not as a pest or an inconvenient endeavor, and we should encourage it at all stages of life for the benefit of every individual and the society at large.

19

Teach the Beauty of Mathematics

What nobler employment, or more valuable to the state, than that of the man who instructs the rising generation?
Cicero

Many people go through life with a dislike of mathematics and even worse, with the so-called 'math anxiety' which hinders many college achievements since most academic programs include a certain degree of mathematics. Over 28 years of teaching I have very rarely encountered math instructors advancing the idea that in fact mathematics is an art and, therefore, we should learn to appreciate its beauty. In this respect, we should not limit the teaching of mathematics only to its usefulness, to applications in the 'real life,' but we should also underline its often elegant ways to solve complex problems. In this respect, instructors of mathematics at all levels should search for best solutions or procedures so that students discover early enough the non-threatening nature of mathematics and its elegance. This way, an intelligent combination of the practical sense of math with its sophistication and often-overlooked simplicity, might bring forth the true beauty of mathematics. As a result, we should expect more candidates dedicated to the challenging commitment of teaching mathematics, which in return will ensure a brighter future for mathematics instruction in the U.S.

In the following I will present a few examples and I encourage math instructors to search for more.

1. <u>Radicals</u>
   Based on properties of rational exponents, we are able to simplify the index of the radical and the exponent of the radicand directly by their greatest common factor, like in this example:
   $$\sqrt[8]{x^6} = \sqrt[4]{x^3}$$
   This prevents extensive work with rational exponents, which work implies several steps to simplify and to write the answer in radical form again. Evidently, this procedure can also be used from right to left: we can multiply both the index of the radical and the exponent of the radicand by the same number. This is very useful when we need to find the least common multiple of indexes of radicals in order to multiply radical expressions. Here is a more complex application:
   $$\sqrt{x}\,(\sqrt[3]{2x} - \sqrt[5]{x^2}) =$$
   $$\sqrt{x} \cdot \sqrt[3]{2x} - \sqrt{x} \cdot \sqrt[5]{x^2} =$$
   $$\sqrt[6]{x^3} \cdot \sqrt[6]{(2x)^2} - \sqrt[10]{x^5} \cdot \sqrt[10]{(x^2)^2} =$$
   $$\sqrt[6]{4x^5} - \sqrt[10]{x^9}$$

2. <u>The Quadratic Formula</u>
   Most of us are familiar with the famous "quadratic formula" used to solve quadratic equations especially when the solutions are irrational or complex numbers. Given the equation $ax^2 + bx + c = 0$, with real coefficients a. b, c, the quadratic formula that solves this equation is:
   $$x = \frac{-b \pm \sqrt{b^2 - 4ac}}{2a}.$$

   Some of us might already know the "half quadratic formula" that uses half of b and it works only when b is an even number, Therefore, it can be used half the time, but, since it involves only half the steps in order to

simplify the answer, is still very useful. Letting p be half of b (p = b/2), the half quadratic formula is:
$$x = \frac{-p \pm \sqrt{p^2 - ac}}{a}.$$

Here is an example that illustrates the benefits (fewer steps) in solving the equation: $3x^2 - 6x + 2 = 0$. Since b = -6, p = -3 and the solution is:
$$x = \frac{-(-3) \pm \sqrt{(-3)^2 - 3 \cdot 2}}{3} = \frac{3 \pm \sqrt{9-6}}{3} = \frac{3 \pm \sqrt{3}}{3}.$$

Otherwise, the solving will take 6-7 steps.

3. Applications

The following is an example of the use of properties of quadratic functions in solving day-by-day application problems.

"Sarah, a life guard, has 100 yards of 'floating rope' to close in a rectangular swimming area for kids. Obviously she will need to use the rope only on the three sides of the rectangle that are on the water. How much should the length and the width of the rectangle be so that Sarah will close in a maximum swimming area?"

Solution:

As we can see on the diagram, if we choose x for the width, the length will be 100 – 2x.

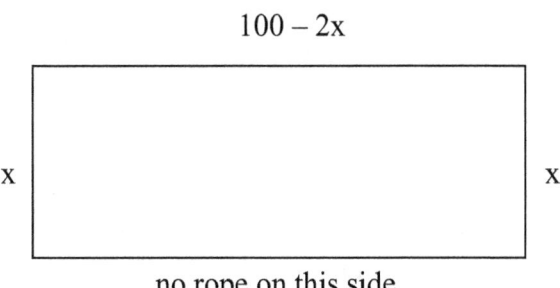

no rope on this side

Since the formula for the area of a rectangle is Area = length · width, on this application we have:
$$A = (100 - 2x)x. \quad (1)$$
We can see, therefore, that this formula for the area is actually a quadratic function that can be written this way:
$$A(x) = -2x^2 + 100x. \quad (2)$$
The classical solution to this problem usually involves finding the vertex of the quadratic function (the concave down parabola which has a maximum value) from equation (2), since the x of the vertex will be the width of the rectangle.

I propose here a simpler and more elegant solution based on properties of the graph of equation (1) (this approach does not even involve equation (2), and it can be obviously used in many other applications). Since a parabola has an axis of symmetry that passes through the vertex, and since we can easily find its x-intercepts from equation (1) that is already in factored form, we can as easily find the midpoint between the x-intercepts. This is exactly where the axis of symmetry is located, which will be the x of the vertex, hence the width of the rectangle.

Setting $(100 - 2x)x = 0$, the x-intercepts are 0 and 50. This means that the x of the vertex is $x = 25$, which is the midpoint of the segment from 0 to 50 (see figure 1 in the appendix 2). Therefore, in order to maximize the swimming area, Sarah needs to set up a rectangle with the width of 25 yards and the length $(100 - 2x)$ of 50 yards (on a lighter note: Sarah's supervisor will be very impressed and will give her a raise).

4. **The Pythagorean Theorem:** $a^2 + b^2 = c^2$

There are hundreds of proofs for this ancient theorem that one can find on the internet, some more complex than others. However, to underline the beauty of mathematics, I would like to present here a very short and clear proof that I stumbled upon recently (Birkhoff, p. 92). It is based on a given right triangle of legs a and b with the hypotenuse c, and three similar triangles to the given one obtained by scaling the original triangle by factors of a, b, and respectively c. Remembering that c is the larger of the three sides, positioning the three resulting similar right triangles as in figure 2 in appendix 2 (the two smaller ones within the larger one) the proof of the theorem is obvious:

$$aa + bb = cc, \text{ or } a^2 + b^2 = c^2.$$

Author at the Versailles museum, France

20

Global Education

I have learned through bitter experience the one supreme lesson to conserve my anger, and as heat conserved is transmitted into energy, even so our anger controlled can be transmitted into a power that can move the world.
Mahatma Gandhi

We are living in a new century and a new millennium. We are in 2011 and the world is more united today than it has been in the known history in spite of the present international conflicts. For better or for worse, technology has helped the virtually instantaneous exchange of information around the world in such a manner that we all *feel* closer together than ever before. The ease of traveling, although international traveling is not cheap, physically makes the world a smaller place than ever before. Consequently, worldwide cultural exchanges, especially after the fall of Communism in Europe, have become more of a norm than a novelty. Businesses expand and spread all around the world, including geographical areas that so far have known a relatively low-level of economical sophistication – see investments in Eastern Europe, for example, and the economical boom of China and India. Now, one can argue whether this is for the betterment of the respective population or in fact it is detrimental, but in the long run the general human progress on Earth *does* include efforts on easing the lives of as many human beings as possible. Historically speaking, the easiness comes from limiting hard labor and making available a variety of choices to satisfy one's basic necessities such as food, clothing, shelter, education, and entertainment.

Teach For Life

As the world evolved into a more global community those who have and live in freedom felt more and more inclined to help those less fortunate and oppressed. For economical and/or humanitarian reasons many governments follow this path, hence, some of the tight situations we have in the world. It is obvious that the educational level dictates the awareness and the flexibility in reasoning of the respective population. Also considering their national tradition, social makeup, cultural inheritance, and their religious philosophy, the integration of some societies into the global environment is very difficult. This is evident especially in the Middle East and somewhat in Eastern Europe.

Assuming that globalization is the way to approach humanity's future, global education comes in as a major factor. By this I mean that some norms in modern education *are in fact universal*. Education should provide *everyone* in the world with the basic understanding and acceptance of the fact that some practices in treating human beings are really not acceptable. In this respect even ancient religious creeds fail the test of what is humane and what is not. Some clear examples speak for themselves: women should not be treated with less dignity than men (voting rights, rights in a court of law, education, and earning equity), children should not be exploited for cheap labor, people should not be indoctrinated into radical theologies that promote martyrdom, freedom of religion should be upheld, and freedom of movement should not be restricted from those who do want to start a new life somewhere else in the world.

As one who has been deprived of true freedom for the first 26 years of his life (living in Communist Romania up to 1981) I can testify to the importance of the free exchange of ideas in the world. The hunger for such exchange we felt during the years of Communism in Romania pushed many to extremes, and I was one of those who decided to defect in 1981. The world opened up to me as my escape route took me through the former Yugoslavia, then Italy, with several months in a political refugee camp, and finally immigrating to the United States of America. Over time I realized that in fact people were people wherever my life took me, with good and bad, with selfish and giving individuals, with rich and poor, and so on. However, the more places I have visited over the years, such as states in the United States (Texas, New York, Florida, Kansas, California, Virginia, Ohio, Louisiana, Alaska), Canada, Mexico, and countries in Europe (Italy, Germany, Greece, Spain, France, England, Hungary, Austria) I arrived at the conclusion that what could help us all human beings on this planet survive in the long run is an education that promotes universal human values in all corners of the world. That excludes dictating to others what they should cherish or not. Instead, it includes moral and ethical norms that are common sense regardless of the nationality and the religious creed of the individual. In this respect people in the position to make decisions in modern global education should respect and closely examine education from other parts of the world in search for *what is constructive* in order to adopt it into their own system. In some academic areas practices elsewhere might be more productive than the ones in place at home. To reject different ideas without a close scrutiny becomes an arrogant and a self-defeating approach in today's global teaching and learning.

Global Education to Global Economy

As we should strive to preserve local and national characteristics in terms of traditions and the production of specific goods (like food and cultural artifacts, for instance), it is more and more evident that the entire world cherishes good imports from everywhere. The variety we find in U.S. stores that educates us about life elsewhere should be available in other parts of the world also; people in Africa or the Middle East should have the opportunity to shop in a U.S.-like grocery store, for example. However, there are still great efforts to block such availability and I experienced it first hand before 1981 in Romania. Out of a sense of pride, rigidity, domination, or ignorance many governments still prohibit the import of culture, education, technology, and strategies for economic development. For usually political and religious reasons true progressive values are rejected, and millions of people are still kept in the dark in respect to the latest achievements around the world. As we in the U.S. enjoy most of such modern accomplishments, so would people in many other countries that are now still oppressed by their governments for previously mentioned reasons.

If we really care about the well-being of people all over the world we should be for democracy and freedom everywhere and we should sponsor this kind of thought under all circumstances. Therefore, dictatorships should be a thing of the past and the rest of the free world should join hands to celebrate and support every little step in this direction. Within this picture of the world education becomes implicitly global and international educational exchanges at all academic levels are a necessity. Let us all be for such exchanges in order to ensure a positive development of the human race on all fronts.

21

Self-leadership For a Better Life

The dedicated life is the life worth living. You must give with your whole heart.
Annie Dillard

Based on my experience in academic institutions and my extensive research, I would like to propose a new perspective on teaching and learning. This new philosophy in education can bring much-needed peace of mind to teachers, students, and parents that still feel stressed out and challenged negatively by events in their lives. Unreasonable expectations, a misunderstanding of natural processes, and a lack of acceptance of circumstances can cause stress and can lead to high levels of anxiety.

In this respect, let us imagine ourselves in the middle of nature. Beautiful woods surround us, the rushing water of a little creek plays its rhythm on a winding course, and on the horizon majestic mountains are striving patiently to reach a cloudless sky with their snow-capped peaks. We are moved by the grandeur of this picture and we don't want it to be any different: a crooked tree shouldn't be straight, the rocks shouldn't be perfectly aligned, and the mountain peaks shouldn't be all identical and uniformly covered by snow and ice. Instead, we accept the view as is because we understand it to be the result of years and years of transformation.

On the other hand, if we sit on a park bench watching people pass by, we start judging and implicitly want them to be different: this person could lose a few pounds, that person could change hair style, another person is too loud, etc. We fail to understand that in fact that is the way they are *at this time*, as a result of years of evolution and transformation.

The beauty of this picture is even greater than that of the previous one because it portrays the result of the most impressive transformation we currently know in the universe: that of a sensitive human being. Why should the human world change in order for us to be happy? Why can't we be happy with the world as it is today? How else can it be *today* since it already evolved to its present state? It is true that we don't want famine, domestic violence, or wars in the world, but we have to realize that this state of affairs is the result of years of human evolution and we should accept it without anxiety and fear, but with hope for a better future. Gandhi suggests that we should become the changes we want to see in the world. Then, if we want peace, love, and prosperity we, ourselves, should become peace, love, and prosperity, leaving fear and anxiety aside, knowing that it all depends on us. The physics of the 20th century, the quantum physics, supports the view of unity and interdependence in the universe. There is a constant exchange of energy that maintains the universal balance. In fact it suggests that the events around us are not as random or accidental as people think. With this understanding in mind we can approach our daily life with a different chosen attitude, learning from the past in order to create a brighter future.

The Academic Field

The future is highly created in the field of education, and this applies to both academic teaching-learning and personal growth. Educators, students, and parents should strive for the best they could be in their relationship to others. This implies continued efforts on self-development and self-leadership. Everything we think, say, and do today has been learned at some point in the past. If we show hate, anger, impatience, and selfishness it is because that is what is inside of us and as we manifest them, so becomes the world around us. However, if we want this world to be characterized by love, patience, kindness, and compassion that is exactly what we should manifest ourselves.

Self-leadership For a Better Life

There are many instructors across all disciplines who have great academic accomplishments but they are unhappy teaching. Their choice of attitudes is to blame students, colleagues, the schedule, and in general, they complain about being victims in an unfair world. It seems to me that they could choose different attitudes, and that they fail to see the deeper reality, namely the fact that in a perfectly balanced universe the circumstances of their lives are caused by their chosen attitudes, actions, and reactions to previous events that had their own causes, which were the effects of other causes, and so on. Those 'problem students' or uncooperative colleagues are not there accidentally! In the larger unseen reality there are precise reasons for those challenges.

We need to remember that we learn something from every encounter, especially from those that are not exactly comfortable. Here is a first-hand example from my classroom. Many years ago I had a student in College Algebra who did not take the course seriously and even disturbed the class several times, making a D at the end of the semester. In spite of my friendly (well-intended) suggestions and help throughout the term, she gave me the worst student-evaluation I have ever received. I did not consider it a major problem but the universe, in its unseen wisdom, made sure justice was done without me having to do *anything*. For the next two semesters this student signed up to retake College Algebra, but she signed up for sections that I will eventually be assigned to teach at the last-minute, without her knowing, since she was desperately trying to run away from me. Needless to say, she made Ds both times, in spite of my complete professional help and cooperation. Eventually, some years later, she stepped over the hurdle and finished Calculus (for the complete story, please see my book WE ARE ALL ONE). Obviously, this encounter shows clearly that we do not have to do anything intentional to 'settle the score' and create more negativity, since the universe takes care of the details within the law of cause and effect that governs both physical and nonphysical reality.

In this respect, to function properly, any system strives for balance. Whenever this balance is affected the system attempts to bring it back at any cost. Nature displays this fact very clearly through earthquakes, storms, fires, etc. Human beings have other options, however. We can use different ways to establish balance in our lives through *understanding*. Sometimes we instinctively release stress, anxiety, and fear explosively, but frequently a true understanding of the way things are as the law of cause and effect dictates, helps us sustain a balanced life with no extra effort at all; that is the way of the greatest masters in history.

Consequently, in the field of education we should not entertain a victimization attitude in any endeavor. The understanding mentioned before should release us also from guilt, as long as we know we do the best we can under any circumstance. Even situations when we know we did not do all we could have done should leave us free of fear and guilt since, in fact, *we know we did not apply ourselves fully*. In other words, as long as we have reasons for the choices we make, leading to ever-improving outcomes of events in our lives, our balance should not be perturbed.

Conclusion

In order to maintain this balance, and therefore, for peace of mind in our lives, I would like to outline a simple and practical strategy. We need to understand that the ancestor of any word, action, or material artifact we produce is a chosen attitude and/or thought. By controlling our thoughts and attitudes we can generate the results we want in our lives. The future comes from the patterns of the present. Nothing happens at random in the universe and this holds true for human life as well. Each of us receives exactly the fruit of what we have created in the past, nothing more, nothing less, whether we remember the causes or not. This realization should help us release fear, tension, stress, regrets, jealousy, sadness, blame, envy, hate, and even meaningless racial and gender discords. Consequently, we will enjoy better teaching and learning conditions, in an atmosphere of acceptance, love, understanding, help, and compassion. The present is the only time when we can apply this new mind-set and the future will follow the pattern we initiate today: it has no other choice.

Enchanted Rock, Texas

22

Question Some Words and Expressions

Worry does not empty tomorrow of its sorrow; it empties today of its strength.
                                               Corrie Ten Boom

In many situations we are at the mercy of the meaning we put into some words or expressions, for good or for bad. In order to eliminate negative effects of the language we use I suggest we abolish some words and expressions or at least restrict their usage as much as possible.

Accidents and Randomness

In a universe governed by the law of cause and effect "accidents" and "randomness" cannot take place. All words and expressions based on these two concepts have no real foundation. For example, if we roll a "perfect" die with 6 faces numbered from 1 to 6 we say that *randomly* we can get any one of the 6 numbers 1/6 of the time. But that is not necessarily true: getting number 5, for instance, is not a "random" event. It is precisely caused by the specific conditions of that particular roll: the face that was up initially, the number of rotations, the surface we use for the experiment, the angle of the spin of the throw, and why not, the "perfection" with which the die was manufactured in the first place – a slight imbalance in the distribution of weight inside the die could favor some sides at the expense of others. Therefore, the outcome is not a "random" outcome, but a very precise effect caused by actual conditions. The problem is the multitude of the actual conditions and a virtual impossibility to study and predict their impact precisely. I can postulate that if we could ensure *exactly* the same conditions we will *always* get the same face of the die as the respective conditions dictate. Here is what Einstein said regarding the lack of accuracy in forecasting the changes in weather: "Occurrences in this domain are beyond the reach of exact prediction because of the variety of factors in operation, not because of any lack of order in nature."

Along the same lines, we say that there was an "accident" at an intersection: two cars collided and two people are dead. If we examine an "accident" closely we cannot but notice that in order for the "accident" to happen, both cars must be in the same place at the same time. If one car was a fraction of a second late or early, it could not happen. If one driver left the gas station a few seconds later or earlier, for example, it could not happen. If one of them traveled slightly faster, it could not happen, etc. Therefore, one could see how the "accident" looks more like an appointment conducted with precision so that both parts are at the right time in the right place for the meeting. Just because we don't always understand the deeper reasons for certain events in our lives it doesn't mean that they happen "accidentally," "randomly," or "chaotically," chaos being just a very complex order, and/or an order we do not yet understand.

Consequently, we should not use "incidentally, coincidentally, randomly" in any situation because they imply that events can take place out of nowhere, without an actual cause. We know that this is completely untrue. On the other hand, assuming it is true, we give power to randomness by considering ourselves powerless. Any chosen attitude may become a self-fulfilling prophecy. Accepting that all events are purely the results of previous causes, offers the comfort of an explanation for their occurrence, which gives us control over how we choose to perceive the situation. As soon as we understand logically that we are not at the mercy of randomness, we should be filled with peace of mind and calm to handle the situations from a much better perspective: one of lucid thinking and not one of "poor me, I am a victim again."

Honestly, to Tell you the Truth!

As soon as I hear such expressions a question comes to my mind: "What do you mean: now you are telling the truth but usually you don't?" How can I trust such a person? The problem starts with the acceptance of the so-called "little lies" that supposedly don't hurt anybody: we know they may. Perhaps it is not a direct, obvious, and immediate "hurt" but most lies are discovered. This is due to, once again, the cause and effect nature of our universe: for every action there is a reaction. By the way, is the person telling the "little lie" really happy about it? I don't think so – and this is already one part of the negative reaction! Another aspect of it is that usually a lie will be followed by many others, most of the time just to cover the first one. Even worse, people who tell "small lies" may tell bigger ones also, since it may become a habit if not an addiction. So I suggest we make a conscious and firm effort to refrain as much as possible from telling lies, and we should abolish the use of such expressions as "Honestly," "To tell you the truth," "The truth is," etc.

Lucky, Unfortunately

This is another theme that springs from the basic cause and effect nature of our universe. In a perfectly balanced system such as our world there is really no room for "fortune" or lack of it: everything happens as a direct or indirect result of its causes. However, we, as the 'smart' human beings we are, like to put an emotional spin on things so we can get some satisfaction out of it. We love the drama of "good luck" or "bad luck" since this gives us a chance to shift the responsibility from ourselves to something else (for example to randomness – sounds familiar?). The negative aspect of this reality is that so many people suffer unnecessarily at the hands of "lady misfortune," forgetting that it is really only a figment of their imagination, in fact the unwanted events being the result of previous actions *they* took. Things happen the way they do as effects of real causes, as they become causes for other things to take place in the future. And the same applies to "good fortune" on the stage of our emotional rollercoaster; we celebrate it as if we did not have anything to do with it (it just happened); how nice to be lucky! Whenever we blame anything other than ourselves, we reduce or remove our own power to correct the problem or at least to explain it.

Consequently, in order to take full charge of our lives we should not play the cards of good or bad fortune, or blame very much at all. Instead, we should accept the outcomes, notice their nature, try to see the situations from different perspectives, and we should not suffer over them. In the same time we should not go overboard with joy or excitement. The higher goal is to minimize the side effects, look for the hidden benefits, and to go on with a balanced and happy life.

Mistakes

We don't know how to make a mistake. We declare a 'mistake' after the fact, but the fact itself is the best we could do at the respective time. We don't wake up in the morning saying: today I will make two mistakes. Instead, we say: oops, I made a mistake, which by definition is a statement that underlines an event that already took place. Even more, at the present time it is out of our control, since we cannot go back in time to fix it. We may be able to take satisfaction from what we learned from those facts.

Therefore, to prevent self-incrimination, which often happens when we identify our mistakes, we should not use the word 'mistake,' or at least we should not use it with this connotation. We should adopt the understanding that all facts are just that, facts, and we should assume the responsibility for the consequences, of course learning from them but not undermining our credibility and self-confidence. We should state the facts (the 'mistakes'), and when we see that our choices were insufficient to meet the challenge of the situation, we should learn from them so that we handle the matter better next time. A possible way to express it might be: "Yes, I am now aware that it wasn't the optimum approach and I know I can do better" or in short "OK, let's do better."

"Hang in There" and "I'm Here"

Many times I greet people with "How are you?" only to get answers like "I'm hanging in there" or "I'm here" as if to say "I am struggling to be here and do what I do but I would rather be somewhere else or do something else." Of course one could argue that at that particular moment in time they don't feel well, hence their attitude. Although it appears logical, I would respond that as long as we are where we want to be and we are doing what we want to do in life, just because we "don't feel too well" it is not an excuse to act and propagate a negative attitude, or a "down and depressed" approach to life. You can have a cold, you might be tired, or even have personal problems and still be and show that you are happy to be where you are and do what you do since it is all the natural result (or effect) of a long chain of your chosen attitudes and previous causes.

Of course, this presupposes in the first place that, ideally, we are where we want to be and we do what we want to do in life. If this is not the case, we better find "where we want to be and what we want to do" instead of just surviving from day-to-day, month-to-month, and year-to-year being where we don't want to be and doing what we don't really want to do. We need to remember that the world does not owe us happiness and fulfillment. *We* are the ones responsible to reach that goal, as we live in the free world where we can exercise our choices. A simple change in attitude might work wonders in many cases just to put a smile on a face that otherwise would be sad and depressed.

T. G. I. F.

Many times we hear this ... on a Friday: "Thank God It's Friday!" This says: "I am so glad the week is over. Here is the weekend – party time!" And that might be exactly how many people feel. However, this expresses clearly that they have not enjoyed their week, that their week was a drag, and in most cases it means that their profession is not something to make them happy. So, I say again, it is up to us to find something we really like doing, so that we can say *every day* "Thank God it is today!" Our happiness is up to us, not to the calendar or the circumstances around us.

On a related idea, statistics show that the largest number of people who die of heart problems is on Monday morning between 8 and 9. Why? The answer seems to be clear: many people hate Monday mornings and, consequently, they put much more pressure and stress on themselves on Mondays than they do the rest of the week; on Fridays they probably are most relaxed. So, we can see how the simple chosen perception of Mondays as the end of a weekend and the beginning of a new week can actually kill people.

As a remedy, we should also see that it is up to us to teach ourselves to perceive all days of the week equally enjoyable. This is not difficult to do when we create a state of mind that allows us to feel good all the time.

Such a state of mind comes naturally when we educate ourselves to choose to see life as a journey full of wonders but not full of traps and victimizing circumstances. As soon as we see ourselves as the creators of our destiny instead of victims of random events, we are free to simply choose to be happy, looking for the benefits of every situation, understanding the larger picture of the universe and our place in it. In this respect one can find great support in the study of ancient spirituality and modern science, especially quantum physics, and the available information on these fields is abundant (see my book, WE ARE ALL ONE).

23

Learn to Love Your Life

Neither a lofty degree of intelligence nor imagination nor both together go to the making of genius. Love, love, love, that is the soul of genius.
Wolfgang Amadeus Mozart

So many times people complain about circumstances in their lives up to the point of hating their own existence. I believe that this reality springs from an understanding of life as a long sequence of events, many of them viewed to be far from people's control and determination. This leads one to interpret such events as victimization attempts during which they are just supposed to suffer at the hands of an undefined providence, hence a feeling of resentment and even hate of their own lives. Since I think that one meaning of our lives is to be happy at nobody's expense, I feel that we can all educate ourselves in that direction. Here is a personal story that can serve as an inspiration to all of us who still struggle with the natural flow of life.

Author's grandfather

I grew up in Romania in the 1950s and 60s and for the first 19 years of my life I was very close to my grandfather on my father's side. We lived in the same household in a small village, so over those years we spent a lot of time together. He was born in 1902 in that village and he never left it for any extended period of time except for the military recruitment during the Second World War. He grew up in a family of peasants (farmers) and as a consequence, combined with economic reasons, he only finished the first 2 grades of education. The rest of his life he spent as a peasant on his own land up to 1962, when the Communist Party nationalized most of the agricultural land and private properties in the country. After that, my grandfather continued his simple life with the rest of the people in the village, but now working for the state on the state-owned land, with nationalized farm animals, machineries, buildings, etc.

Ever since I started walking he took me out in the fields, had me ride horses, and this way I have been acquainted with most of the farming activities, which I like even today. I developed an appreciation for gardening, for green grass, for the smell of fresh hay, for the woods, for fruit trees, and I enjoyed a closeness to horses, water buffalos, sheep, lambs, pigs, dogs, and chickens.

This was in fact my grandfather's entire life: wake up at dawn and go to bed at dark, after occasionally having a drink or reading the newspaper and sometimes a bit from the Bible. Since radio and television sets were available only in the mid '60s to such communities in Romania, his time was very efficiently divided almost exclusively between agricultural activities, such that at the end of the harvest season the family will be provided for for an entire year. Sundays would be church days with very welcome chances to socialize after the religious mass and chat with others about communal issues.

Under these circumstances his life was mainly centered in his hometown, closely interacting with other people, with neighbors, with the few relatives he could claim, and working close to exhaustion almost every day. I hardly remember a few times when my grandfather visited a city, most of these memories coming from the wonderful bedside stories he used to tell me when I was little. However, he was very aware of the world outside the village from many sources, but he never expressed any regret for not being able to travel more, have more, know more, accomplish more, or be more. He seemed to be a happy person most of the time, content with living his life to the fullest within the obvious limits, and never complaining or claiming to be a victim of circumstances. Occasionally he would sing folkloric repertory he had learned by ear over the years, either at work for small audiences of friends, relatives, or coworkers, or simply alone while performing certain tasks around the house. On one single occasion I took advantage of a borrowed reel-to-reel recorder and taped about 20 minutes of his singing at the end of a hard day of work in the fields: it is and it will remain a treasure forever!

In December 1974 my grandfather died at the end of about a week of sickness, the only extended period of time for which I ever remember him to be incapacitated. On his deathbed he uttered one of the most profound sentences I have ever heard. He said it kindly, with regret in his soft voice: "I will be missing this world very much!"

For many years I have been thinking of this statement as an appropriate measure of appreciation for our own lives: my grandfather loved his life even as limited and unilateral as it was. He didn't say: "I wish I did" this or that. Instead, he just affirmed that he will be missing the world he knew and the life he led because he loved them. Now, in retrospective, I understand even better his love for singing and entertaining the ones around him: he really liked to be alive and to do what he was doing, most of the time regardless of the circumstances. The attitudes he chose served him and his family very well.

As I bring this idea to the present, it is even more important to us in the West, today, in this world of all possibilities, with the freedom and easiness to travel, and with all the information we desire at our fingertips, to treasure what we have and to be thrilled to be alive. Moreover, at least in the U.S. we have all doors open to education, and especially to higher education by means of community colleges and universities. We know how important education is and how we can fulfill our dreams through education. If my grandfather enjoyed his life as it was - simple and linear, with little education - what real reasons do we have today not to enjoy ours, since we can take advantage of such a variety of sources of excitement and fulfillment?

One possible reason could be that more and more people in the modern world learn not to appreciate the little things; they don't stop to smell the roses, so to speak. In this respect my grandfather did have a great appreciation for the little events and accomplishments around his home and didn't spend too much energy on dreaming about out-of-reach endeavors. This can be another reason why today so many people fall prey to unhappiness: under an advertisement bombardment to get more, to be more, to accomplish more, they place themselves in competition with a certain standard that in many cases is out of reach. Consequently, the failure to accomplish those illusory goals can be the cause for unhappiness, unworthiness, depression, and in the end for the deep feeling that their entire life is a waste.

Happiness is not "out there" and we have to get it. It is within, and we just have to *be* it. After all, there are so many people happy with very little, as there are a lot of rich people totally unhappy. Some claim that people are "wired" to be or not to be happy. However, I believe that the "wiring" can be manipulated through education and recognition of choices. So, in many cases a change in the personal philosophy and understanding of life could dramatically bring people closer to a state of happiness than anything else. The volume of publications on "self-development" or "self-growth" is impressive, and that makes our quest for happiness much more manageable, which is the purpose of this essay.

Yes, we can be happy, regardless of the circumstances, and we can learn to love our lives by finding what we really like to occupy our time with, or we can learn to love what we do. My grandfather did it almost to perfection as he made himself a functional part of the community. This implies a departure from the rigid, impractical, dogmatic, and doctrinal paradigm that permeates the modern Western world. In this respect, we need to remove ourselves from the victimization and separation model sustained by the practice of senseless discrimination and competition. As soon as we can see ourselves as integral, meaningful components of a larger whole within a natural order, the separation anxiety will vanish, leaving room for inner peace and, why not, for happiness and love of life.

24

Teach Life's Real Values

It is not the brains that matter most, but that which guides them – the character, the heart, generous qualities, progressive ideas.
Fyodor Dostoyevsky

Moral and ethical norms are determined and set in place by the general popular philosophical convictions promoted by the society. Such convictions spring from the level of individual acceptance of the respective philosophical concepts. The social group that helps materialize this acceptance is composed of all active providers of education. Families, schools, churches, places of employment, and entertainment establishments join hands in shaping the essential set of practical moral and ethical values of the individual. However, none of the aforementioned educational providers can "teach" values which are not *already* part of their present existential philosophy; or in other words, one cannot teach something one does not know. Therefore, we can clearly see that within a picture of separation between the material and the spiritual makeup of the universe, the values that will be promoted will follow suit. That is why we witness today in the Western world the manifestation of a set of values that mirror this separation philosophy within every area of human endeavor. The ego drives people to selfish acts of survival (much like in the animal kingdom) based on an existential philosophy that maintains the idea of separation from God (or the spiritual universe) and also separation from nature. This separation is indeed an illusion caused by the limited perception human beings experience via the five basic physical senses: seeing, hearing, smelling, touching, and tasting.

Warning!

The history of the human race shows clearly that, as civilizations base their existential philosophy on the survival and expansion instinct, they will destroy other civilizations in the process. Moreover, the danger is also that the expanding civilizations, not having solved their existential problems at home, will infiltrate them into those whom they conquer. The discovery and occupation of the Americas, when the Inca, Aztec, Maya, and the North American native civilization have been virtually eliminated, come to mind.

In this respect, a warning is in order. This warning does not only pertain to earthly expansion and occupation. As the 21st century human race aspires to extraterrestrial contact, we should be more concerned with the solving of our existential problems at home. First, attain a balanced and universal philosophy of life based on real values, and only then attempt any kind of expansion. We should learn from our history, not repeat it.

Teach the Value of Non-addiction

Since 'who we are we carry with us everywhere we go,' we also need to remember that all humans are beings of habit. From young to old, as we sufficiently repeat a certain task, it becomes part of our memory, our ability, and, why not, our preference. That is the truth behind the famous saying in education: "Repetition is the mother of all learning."

However, this fact of life is a double edge sword. Repetition doesn't only help the learning of positive traits as part of constructive education, but it can also make people addicted to unhealthy habits such as drinking, smoking, drugs, gambling, and so on. Consequently, we should practice and teach a philosophy of non-addiction. The best prevention is complete abstinence; not even one step should be taken towards a practice that we very well know it to be detrimental. In this respect, non-addiction implies a life of true freedom and happiness without the need of a regular 'fix,' and it should fit well with other higher moral and ethical values we treasure.

Real Values

Let us examine now which moral and ethical values should really matter. It is evident that the human race has been searching for such traits regardless of the historical and geographical scene. All religions and spiritual traditions show a path of discovery, testing and implementing moral and ethical standards. From time to time, whenever a logical and common sense understanding of a norm is missing, strict laws are passed in order to impose social acceptance and compliance. The values in need of such regulation, since they are frequently trespassed, show the fruit of the scientific and religious doctrine of separation versus that of union and interconnection.

Here is one simple example. Many people are convinced that, under special circumstances, it is okay to lie. Upon a close inspection, indeed we realize that telling the truth is the one most frequently broken ethical law. In all walks of life, from small and seemingly unimportant personal situations to international political intrigues, people often hide the truth. Even under oath some individuals think that their cause is more important than telling the truth (one can find many examples from the political arena and the corporate world). Why? Why some people think that if they are not caught telling a lie, everything is well? The answer to this question is given by the education these people received. From families, relatives, and friends, to churches, academic institutions, and the military, the message put forth by individuals of high moral and ethical standards is not able to convince *all* people that it is better to tell the truth. Within a model of universal interconnection I suggest that lying to others is not only undermining one self's credibility but also may create negative self repercussions in the future (what goes around comes around). After all, would we, *ourselves*, like to be lied to? However, I understand that in a less than perfect world there are circumstances that might justify lying in order to prevent much worse, or even deadly outcomes. In the same time, though, I am of the opinion that we need to strive for the implementation of highest moral and ethical values if we aspire to a brighter future ("the problem is not that we set our goals too high and we don't reach them; it is that we set them too low, and we do" - provided we accept the outcomes).

I would like to focus now on the nature of the real values that should guide our lives. What we should consider real norms are those that build an unshakable human character throughout one's life. Real values must be those which are effective regardless of one's material possessions, age, race, nationality, gender, religious belief, or political conviction. Real values are those that do not fluctuate according to our immediate interests. Real values should keep people happy, together, within an atmosphere of healthy and constructive interpersonal relationships. They should manifest within families, within groups of friends sharing interests, within religious and political configurations, within any kind of professional establishment, and should be an integral part of any interaction between total strangers. Real values should be timeless and unconditional, yet subject to continuous improvement, leading to positivity, peace, and hope for a better world.

Besides honesty, the value that impacts our lives the most is love. As we examine different areas of human existence, we notice that wherever love is present, people stay together, live in harmony, work much more productively than otherwise, and interact in positive and efficient ways with each other. It is not an accident that most marriages are based on love, which clearly reflects that love unites, while its opposite, or the lack of love, separates and estranges people. Another obvious example of the manifestation of love is the instinctive affection of parents for their children. It is this kind of love that keeps families together, united within the supreme goal of mutual happiness.

Anywhere the material side of life is dominant, love often appears as a norm conditioned by outcomes of events external to the direct human interaction. Many pretend to love others *if*, and then they list conditions. Many loving relationships start with promises of forever, but after a while something happens and that love cannot be preserved without some fulfilled conditions. Why? Why do people change their perception of love so often and so drastically? An answer can be the fact that many people do not know who they really are (intricate cells in the body of the universe), instead being educated within a philosophy of separation and competition.

Besides honesty and love, here is a list of other human traits that we should all cherish: patience, understanding the needs of others, humility, affection, compassion, charity, modesty, responsibility, and forgiveness. We witness here an understanding of love and compassion as manifestations of the universal side of human existence. However, the doctrine of separation, which is the Western existential paradigm, makes the practical implementation of such a high standard of human behavior difficult. People, more often than not, admire and recognize high norms, but find it hard to effectively assimilate them in their everyday lives. Consequently, the opposites of the desirable human values prevail in many cultural environments, from the personal, which might appear insignificant, to families, communities, and finally, to all of society. It is evident that over the last few decades, although our society made obvious technological and economic progress, the implementation of higher moral and ethical values could have vastly improved. It seems that many people have been neglecting exactly those values which make them human. It also appears that the general pursuit of a higher material living standard has blinded many, causing their ethical and moral values not to improve and in some cases to slip to lower levels.

Explanations and Solutions

Why do some people behave in such unacceptable fashion? The answer should be obvious: the present view of the world, the educational paradigm of separation is not effective enough to convince *all of us* of the paramount importance of proper behavior. Requesting people to adopt high moral and ethical standards only for fear of legal or religious punishment is not the right way and it has been proven ineffective. Even more, in spite of unprecedented technological and economic development, education still has opportunities for substantial improvement. By this I don't mean that technology and financial resources have not been made available in modern education; indeed they are available. Rather, education has not yet evolved into a more efficient human endeavor, capable of explaining the place we really occupy in the universe. The explosion of technology of the last 30 years and new trends in modern education, have greatly impacted teaching and learning in the new Millennium. Within a society ruled by technology, striving exclusively for material gain results in neglecting some of the most common-sense ethical and moral norms of behavior.

The solution we are seeking should be incorporated in modern education under a new paradigm of union. This could be the real treatment for any type of crime and environmental abuse; even better, *real* education, the common sense education that explains the *reasons* for certain social and existential ethical and moral values will actually *prevent* detrimental activities from happening in the first place, just as preventive care is encouraged in medicine. However, people need to be presented with logical evidence in order to incorporate the components of such a "preventive" attitude. This is exactly the core of the new educational paradigm I propose as a model of logical thinking that applies to all walks of life. Quantum physics together with ancient Eastern existential philosophy, personal experience, and common sense bring solid testimonies to the unity of all things, and the documentation is abundant. When all people are aware that *we are all one*, united at a much grander level than we have been taught, people would not strike at others. Convinced of this reality, parents will be able to teach it to their children from day one, educational institutions will widely incorporate it in their curriculum, and, once generalized, people will live as one in all their interactions.

Teach Life's Real Values

As a contrast to such a positive picture, the present model of separation suggests a dim future. Statistics, paired with our firsthand experience, show little or no improvement in the crime rate over the last few decades. Therefore, many of the educational efforts, though positively intended, have been essentially wasted.

There must be a better way. That better way - the solution - is the implementation of the paradigm of union as the basis to the understanding and the living of our lives responsibly at a much higher standard of moral and ethical norms. In this respect, referring to the human condition, Mihai Eminescu (1850-1889), the greatest Romanian poet, states it best in *Scrisoarea I* (The First Letter): "He is in all men, as she is in all women." We see once again that the unity model is being suggested as a solution to all human problems.

25

Exceptional Educational Experiences

Never regard your study as a duty, but as the enviable opportunity to learn to know the liberating influence of beauty in the realm of the spirit for your own personal joy and to the profit of the community to which your later work belongs.
Albert Einstein

    This essay is for you, the reader, to write. Of course, it is a volunteering endeavor for which I leave the next few pages blank. I invite you to recall one exceptional educational experience that significantly marked your life, and write it by hand as essay # 25 in your copy of "Teach for Life." If you agree to share it with me via email I would love to include it in my collection (ir_gl@yahoo.com, please use the subject name "EEE"). Provided I receive enough responses, and of course, with your written permission included in the email or choosing "anonymous," I will select them and I will edit a volume entitled "Exceptional Educational Experiences: True Stories that Can Change Your Life." This volume will offer inspirational examples of educational encounters in order to help motivate others in their pursuit of a better life.
    Thank you for your collaboration, and I wish you well!

About the Author

Irie Glajar was born in Communist Romania in 1955, has graduated from the University of Cluj, Romania, in 1979 with a pre-doctoral degree in Mathematics and Computer Science, and defected from the Communist regime in 1981. After several months in an Italian political refugee camp he immigrated to the United States of America and since September 1982 has been teaching undergraduate mathematics at both high school and college levels in Austin, Texas. Over the years he has participated and presented at many professional conferences in the U.S.A., Canada, and Romania and published several educational articles on modern education. After the 2008 publication of his book "WE ARE ALL ONE, The End of All Worries: Scientific and Spiritual Testimonies to the Unity of all Things," the author focused on research for the present book, "TEACH FOR LIFE, Essays on Modern Education for Teachers, Students, and Parents." Besides enjoying his family life and his teaching career at the Austin Community College, Austin, Texas, Irie Glajar finds much satisfaction in hobbies such as music, gardening, pets, and sports. He is also deeply interested in metaphysics, religion, spirituality, and international traveling, which provide constant inspiration to his teaching of mathematics and to his philosophy of modern education.

Appendix 1

Mathematics Entrance Exam to University – Romania, 1980
(For admission to the 4-year higher education Diploma de Licenta in Mathematics, a post Baccalaureate and pre-doctoral degree program)

Published by Editura Stiintifica si Enciclopedica in 1984, translated into English by the author, from a Romanian collection of math, physics, and chemistry problems.

a) <u>Algebra</u>

1) Show that for $n \geq 10$, $n \in N$, $2^n > n^3$

2) Determine $m \in R$ so that for any $x \in R$ the following is true:
$$(m+1)e^{-2x} + 2(m+1)e^{-x} + m > 0$$

3) Find the polynomial of the smallest degree whose roots are all nonzero complex numbers z, so that $z^2 = \bar{z}$.

4) Let $k \in Q$ (rational numbers) and H be the set of real numbers which can be written in the form $a + b\sqrt{2}$, with $a, b \in Q$, so that $a^2 - kb^2 = 1$. Find a positive integer value of k so that H is a stable part over multiplication.

5) Show that the real number $\log_5 10$ is not rational.

b) **Elements of Mathematical Analysis**

1) Let (a_n) be the sequence defined by $a_1 = 0$, $a_2 = 1$, $a_n = \frac{a_{n-2}}{2} + \frac{a_{n-1}}{2}$, for $n \geq 3$. Show that:

   $a_n = \frac{2}{3}(1 + \frac{(-1)^n}{2^{n-1}})$ for any $n \geq 2$ and determine if the sequence (a_n) converges.

2) Let $f : R - \{0,1\} \to R$ be a function defined by

   $f(x) = \frac{1}{-e + e^{\frac{1}{x}}}$. Determine if the limits at 1 and 0 exist.

3) Determine the real numbers a, b, c, so that:
   $\lim_{n \to \infty} n(an + \sqrt{2 + bn + cn^2}) = 1$.

4) Find the asymptotes of the function

   $f : R - \{\frac{3}{2}\} \to R$ defined by $f(x) = \frac{\sqrt{x^2+1}}{2x-3}$.

5) Let $f : (-\frac{1}{2}, \infty) \to R$ be a function defined by

   $f(x) = \frac{x}{2} \int_0^1 \frac{dt}{(1+tx)\sqrt{1+2tx}}$. Show that

   $f(x) = \arctan\sqrt{1 + 2x} - \frac{\pi}{4}$ for any $x > -\frac{1}{2}$, and evaluate the area between the graph of the function, the x-axis, and limited by the lines $x = 0$ and $x = 1$.

c) **Plane Geometry, Three-dimensional Geometry, Analytic Geometry, and Trigonometry**

1) Show that in any right triangle ABC, the sum of the legs is equal to the sum of the diameters of the circles inscribed and circumscribed to the triangle.

Appendix

2) Show that the projections of two lines on a plane that is parallel to a line that is perpendicular to both given lines, are parallel; discussion.

3) Show that if $x \in (0, \frac{\pi}{2})$, then $sin^2 x + csc^2 x > 2$.

4) Let A and B be two distinctive points in the plane π. Let M be the set of points in π non-collinear with A and B. Let $f : M \to M$ be the function that associates each point $P \in M$ to the orthocenter $f(P)$ of the triangle ABP.

a) Determine the subsets of points P of M, for which $f(P) = C$, where C is any point on the line AB, excluding A and B.

b) Let circle O be in the plane π such that it contains the points A and B. Show that for any point $P \in O \cap M$, $f(P)$ is on circle O', which is symmetrical to circle O about the line AB (analytical solutions are accepted).

Appendix 2

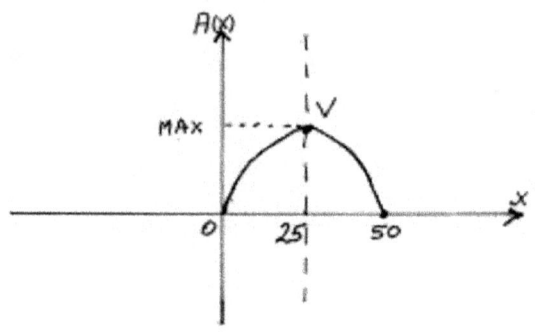

FIGURE 1

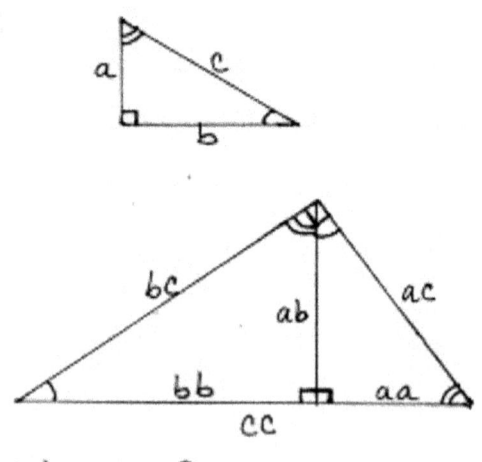

FIGURE 2

www.ingramcontent.com/pod-product-compliance
Lightning Source LLC
Chambersburg PA
CBHW071702040426
42446CB00011B/1868